TO

FROM

THE GREAT HOUSE OF GOD

I cry out to the Lord; I pray to the Lord for mercy.

PSALM 142:1

You can talk to God because God listens. Your voice matters in heaven. He takes you very seriously. When you enter his presence, he turns to you to hear your voice. No need to fear that you will be ignored. Even if you stammer or stumble, even if what you have to say impresses no one, it impresses God, and he listens. Intently. Carefully.

JANUARY 1

WHEN GOD WHISPERS YOUR NAME

Here is a place of rest; let the tired people come and rest.
This is a place of peace.

ISAIAH 28:12

It's quiet. The world is still asleep. In a few moments the day will arrive. For the next twelve hours I will be exposed to the day's demands. It is now that I must make a choice. Because of Calvary, I'm free to choose. And so I choose: Love, joy, peace, patience, kindness, goodness, faithfulness, gentleness, and self-control. To these I commit my day. If I succeed, I will give thanks. If I fail, I will seek his grace. And then, when this day is done, I will place my head on my pillow and rest.

DECEMBER 31

WHEN CHRIST COMES

*D*o you ever feel unnoticed? New clothes and styles may help
for a while. But if you want permanent change, learn to see yourself
as God sees you: "He has covered me with clothes of salvation
and wrapped me with a coat of goodness, like a bridegroom dressed
for his wedding, like a bride dressed in jewels" (Isaiah 61:10).
The challenge is to remember that. To meditate on it.
To focus on it. To allow his love to change the way
you look at you.

JANUARY 2

A GENTLE THUNDER

I leave you peace; my peace I give you. I do not give it to you as the world does. So don't let your hearts be troubled or afraid.

JOHN 14:27

If only you knew that I came to help and not condemn. If only you knew that tomorrow will be better than today. If only you knew the gift I have brought: eternal life. If only you knew I want you safely home.... What wistful words to come from the lips of God.... If only we knew to trust. Trust that God is in our corner. Trust that God wants what is best.

DECEMBER 30

IN THE GRIP OF GRACE

We worry. We worry about the IRS and the SAT and the FBI....
We worry that we won't have enough money, and when we have
money we worry that we won't manage it well. Honestly, now.
Would he teach you to walk just to watch you fall? Would he be
nailed to the cross for your sins and then disregard your prayers?
Come on. Is Scripture teasing us when it reads, "He has put his angels
in charge of you to watch over you wherever you go" (Psalm 91:11)?

I don't think so either.

JANUARY 3

JUST LIKE JESUS

All I have is yours, and all you have is mine.
And my glory is shown through them.

JOHN 17:10

Our goal is not to make our faces radiant. Not even Jesus did that. Matthew says, "Jesus' appearance was changed" not "Jesus changed his appearance."...
Our goal is simply to stand before God with a prepared and willing heart and then let God do his work. And he does. He wipes away the tears. He mops away the perspiration. He softens our furrowed brows. He touches our cheeks. He changes our faces as we worship.

DECEMBER 29

JUST LIKE JESUS

*You will know that God's power is very great
for us who believe.*

EPHESIANS 1:19

God loves to decorate.... Let him live long enough in a heart, and that heart will begin to change. Portraits of hurt will be replaced by landscapes of grace.... This might explain some of the discomfort in your life. Remodeling of the heart is not always pleasant. We don't object when the Carpenter adds a few shelves, but he's been known to gut the entire west wing. He has such high aspirations for you.... He wants you to be just like Jesus.

JANUARY 4

HE STILL MOVES STONES

They all continued praying together with some women,
including Mary the mother of Jesus, and Jesus' brothers.

ACTS 1:14

God has proven himself as a faithful father. Now it falls to us to be trusting
children. Let God give you what your family doesn't. Let him fill the void others
have left. Rely upon him for your affirmation and encouragement. Look at Paul's
words: "you are God's child, and God will give you the blessing he promised,
because you are his child" (Galatians 4:7).

DECEMBER 28

HE STILL MOVES STONES

Is anything too hard for the Lord? No!

GENESIS 18:14

The God of surprises strikes again.... God does that for the faithful.
Just when the womb gets too old for babies, Sarai gets pregnant.
Just when the failure is too great for grace, David is pardoned....
The lesson? Three words. Don't give up.... God is watching.
For all you know right at this moment...the check may be in the mail....
The job contract may be on the desk. Don't quit. For if you do,
you may miss the answer to your prayers.

JANUARY 5

GOD CAME NEAR

He gave up his place with God and made himself nothing. He was born to be a man and became like a servant.

PHILIPPIANS 2:7

It all happened in a most remarkable moment...a moment like no other.... God became a man. Divinity arrived. Heaven opened herself and placed her most precious one in a human womb. The omnipotent, in one instant, became flesh and blood. The one who was larger than the universe became a microscopic embryo. And he who sustains the world with a word chose to be dependent upon the nourishment of a young girl.
God had come near.

DECEMBER 27

THE GREAT HOUSE OF GOD

If people love me, they will obey my teaching.
My father will love them, and we will come to them
and make our home with them.

JOHN 14:23

God wants to be your dwelling place. He has no interest in being a weekend getaway or a Sunday bungalow…. He wants you under his roof now and always…. For many this is a new thought. We think of God as a deity to discuss, not a place to dwell…. But our Father wants…to be the one in whom "we live and move and have our being" (Acts 17:28 NIV).

JANUARY 6

WHEN GOD WHISPERS YOUR NAME

Joseph was the husband of Mary, and Mary was the mother of Jesus. Jesus is called the Christ.

MATTHEW 1:16

Seems like the only common bond between [Jesus' not-so-great grandparents] was a promise. A promise from heaven that God would use them to send his son. Why...does God tell us their stories?... Simple.... He wants us to know that when the world goes wild, he stays calm. Want proof? Read the last name on the list [of Jesus' lineage].... The last name on the list is the first one promised—Jesus. No more names are listed. No more are needed.

DECEMBER 26

THE APPLAUSE OF HEAVEN

*Therefore, there is now no condemnation for those
who are in Christ Jesus.*

ROMANS 8:1 NIV

*F*or those in Christ...you are guaranteed that your sins will be
filtered through, hidden in, and screened out by the sacrifice of Jesus.
When God looks at you, he doesn't see you; he sees the One who
surrounds you. That means that failure is not a concern for you.
Your victory is secure.

JANUARY 7

IN THE GRIP OF GRACE

God shows his great love for us in this way: Christ died for us while we were still sinners.

ROMANS 5:28

"Can anything make me stop loving you?" God asks. "Watch me speak your language, sleep on your earth, and feel your hurts.... You wonder how long my love will last? Find your answer on a splintered cross, on a craggy hill. That's me you see up there, your maker, your God, nail-stabbed and bleeding. Covered in spit and sin-soaked. That's your sin I'm feeling. That's your death I'm dying. That's your resurrection I'm living. That's how much I love you."

DECEMBER 25

A GENTLE THUNDER

*He poured water into a bowl and began
to wash the followers' feet.*

JOHN 13:5

To place our feet in the basin of Jesus is to place the filthiest parts
of our lives into his hands.... He will wash the grimiest part of your life.
If you let him. The water of the Servant comes only when we confess
that we are dirty.... And we will never be able to wash the feet of those who
have hurt us until we allow Jesus, the one we have hurt, to wash ours.

JANUARY 8

THE GREAT HOUSE OF GOD

Thanks be to God for his gift that is too wonderful for words.

2 CORINTHIANS 9:15

I've seen you searching for a gift.... I'm not talking about the obligatory gifts....
I'm talking about that extra-special person and that extra-special gift....
Why do you do it?... You do it so the heart will stop.... You do it to hear
those words of disbelief, "You did this for me?"... And that is why God did it.
Next time a sunrise steals your breath or a meadow of flowers leaves you
speechless, remain that way. Say nothing and listen as heaven whispers,
"Do you like it? I did it just for you."

DECEMBER 24

IN THE EYE OF THE STORM

We have no superhuman High Priest to whom our weaknesses are unintelligible—he himself has shared fully in all our experience of temptation, except that he never sinned (Hebrews 4:15 PHILLIPS).

It's as if he knows that we will say to God...: "God, it's easy for you up there. You don't know how hard it is from down here."

So he boldly proclaims Jesus' ability to understand. Look at the wording again. He himself.... Not an emissary, but Jesus himself. Shared fully. Not partially.... In all our experience.... Why? So he could sympathize with our weaknesses.

JANUARY 9

IN THE GRIP OF GRACE

*He called you to share in his glory in Christ, a glory
that will continue forever.*

1 PETER 5:10

God is willing to forgive all. He's willing to wipe the slate completely clean.
He guides us to a pool of mercy and invites us to bathe. Some plunge in,
but others just touch the surface. They leave feeling unforgiven.... Where the
grace of God is missed, bitterness is born. But where the grace of God
is embraced, forgiveness flourishes.... The more we immerse ourselves
in grace, the more likely we are to give grace.

DECEMBER 23

WHEN GOD WHISPERS YOUR NAME

My kingdom does not belong to this world.

JOHN 18:36

*U*nhappiness on earth cultivates a hunger for heaven. By gracing us with a deep dissatisfaction, God holds our attention. The only tragedy, then, is to be satisfied prematurely. To settle for earth.... We are not happy here because we are not at home here.... And you will never be completely happy on earth simply because you were not made for earth. Oh, you will have your moments of joy.... But they simply do not compare with the happiness that lies ahead.

JANUARY 10

THE APPLAUSE OF HEAVEN

You took away my clothes of sadness, and clothed me in happiness.

PSALM 30:11

The first step to joy is a plea for help.... Those who taste God's presence have declared spiritual bankruptcy and are aware of their spiritual crisis.... They ask God to do for them what they can't do without him. They have seen how holy God is and how sinful they are and have agreed with Jesus' statement, "Salvation is impossible." Oh, the irony of God's delight.... Admission of failure is not usually admission into joy.... But then again, God has never been governed by what is common.

DECEMBER 22

THE GIFT FOR ALL PEOPLE

The Son of Man came to find lost people and save them.

LUKE 19:10

*O*ur God is the God who follows.... Have you felt his presence
through the kindness of a stranger?... Through a word well spoken
or a touch well timed, have you sensed him?...
God gives us himself. Even when we choose our hovel over
his house and our trash over his grace, still he follows....
He uses all his power to convince us that he is who he is
and he can be trusted to lead us home.

JANUARY 11

IN THE GRIP OF GRACE

Those who find me find life, and the Lord will be pleased with them.

PROVERBS 8:35

Grace is created by God and given to man.... On the basis of this point alone, Christianity, is set apart from any other religion in the world.... Every other approach to God is a bartering system; if I do this, God will do that. I'm either saved by works (what I do), emotions (what I experience), or knowledge (what I know). By contrast, Christianity has no whiff of negotiation at all. Man is not the negotiator; indeed, man has no grounds from which to negotiate.

DECEMBER 21

HE STILL MOVES STONES

Martha was distracted with much serving.... But Mary has chosen that good part, which will not be taken away from her.

LUKE 10:40-42 NKJV

*M*artha is worried about something good. She's having Jesus over for dinner. She's literally serving God. Her aim was to please Jesus. But she made a common, yet dangerous mistake...her work became more important than her Lord. What began as a way to serve Jesus, slowly and subtly became a way to serve self.... It's easy to forget who is the servant and who is to be served.

JANUARY 12

THE APPLAUSE OF HEAVEN

Today your Savior was born in the town of David.
He is Christ, the Lord.

LUKE 2:11

*A*n ordinary night with ordinary sheep and ordinary shepherds. And were it not for a God..., the night would have gone unnoticed.... But God dances amidst the common. And that night he did a waltz. The black sky exploded with brightness.... The night was ordinary no more. The angel came in the night because that is when lights are best seen and that is when they are most needed. God comes into the common for the same reason. His most powerful tools are the simplest.

DECEMBER 20

THE GREAT HOUSE OF GOD

*Pray and ask God for everything you need,
always giving thanks.*

PHILIPPIANS 4:6

*H*eaven knows no difference between Sunday morning and Wednesday afternoon. God longs to speak as clearly in the workplace as he does in the sanctuary. He longs to be worshiped when we sit at the dinner table and not just when we come to his communion table. You may go days without thinking of him, but there's never a moment when he's not thinking of you.

JANUARY 13

IN THE GRIP OF GRACE

Every good action and every perfect gift is from God.
These good gifts come down from the Creator of the sun, moon,
and stars, who does not change like their shifting shadows.

JAMES 1:17

The conclusion is unavoidable: self-salvation simply does not work. Man has no way to save himself. But Paul announces that God has a way. Where man fails God excels. Salvation comes from heaven downward, not earth upward. "Every good action and every perfect gift is from God" (James 1:17). Please note: Salvation is God-given, God-driven, God-empowered, and God-originated. The gift is not from man to God. It is from God to man.

DECEMBER 19

JUST LIKE JESUS

In your lives you must think and act like Christ Jesus.
PHILIPPIANS 2:5

God loves you just the way you are, but he refuses to leave you that way.
He wants you to be just like Jesus. God loves you just the way you are.
If you think his love for you would be stronger if your faith were
[stronger], you are wrong.... Don't confuse God's love with the love
of people. The love of people often increases with performance
and decreases with mistakes. Not so with God's love. He loves
you right where you are.

JANUARY 14

THE APPLAUSE OF HEAVEN

God is against the proud, but he gives grace to the humble.

JAMES 4:6

A small cathedral outside Bethlehem marks the supposed birthplace of Jesus. Behind a high altar in the church is a cave.... You can...enter the quiet cave where a star embedded in the floor recognizes the birth of the King. There is one stipulation, however. You have to stoop. The door is so low you can't go in standing up. The same is true of the Christ. You can see the world standing tall, but to witness the Savior, you have to get [down] on your knees.

DECEMBER 18

WHEN CHRIST COMES

Every good action and every perfect gift is from God.
JAMES 1:17

Just look at the gifts [God] has given you: He has sent his angels to care
for you, his Holy Spirit to dwell in you, his church to encourage you,
and his word to guide you.... Anytime you speak, he listens;
make a request and he responds.... As much as you want to see him,
he wants to see you more.... You have been chosen by Christ....
He has claimed you as his beloved.

JANUARY 15

WHEN CHRIST COMES

Here I am! I stand at the door and knock.

REVELATION 3:20

*J*esus goes from heart to heart, asking if he might enter.... Every so often, he is welcomed. Someone throws open the door of his or her heart and invites him to stay. And to that person Jesus gives this great promise:..."In my father's house are many rooms."... What a delightful promise he makes us! We make room for him in our hearts, and he makes room for us in his house.

DECEMBER 17

A GENTLE THUNDER

*God will always give what is right to his people who cry
to him night and day, and he will not be slow
to answer them.*

LUKE 18:7

*W*hy does God wait until the money is gone? Why does he wait
until the sickness has lingered? Why does he choose to wait until the
other side of the grave to answer the prayers for healing? I don't know.
I only know his timing is always right.... With God there are no accidents.
Every incident is intended to bring us closer to him.

JANUARY 16

THE GREAT HOUSE OF GOD

For God did not send His Son into the world to condemn the world, but that the world through Him might be saved.

JOHN 3:17

Can you imagine prospective parents saying, "We'd like to adopt Johnny, but first we want to know [if he has] a few things...." No agency would stand for such talk. Its representative would...say, "...You don't adopt Johnny because of what he has; you adopt him because of what he needs. He needs a home." The same is true with God. He doesn't adopt us because of what we have.... Adoption is something we receive, not something we earn.

DECEMBER 16

WHEN CHRIST COMES

This body that dies must clothe itself with something that can never die.

1 CORINTHIANS 15:53

[Does] Jesus care what clothes we wear? Apparently so. In fact, the Bible tells us exactly the wardrobe God desires. "You were all baptized into Christ, and so you were all clothed with Christ" (Galatians 3:26). This clothing has nothing to do with dresses and jeans and suits. God's concern is with our spiritual garment. He offers a heavenly robe that only heaven can see and only heaven can give.

JANUARY 17

WHEN GOD WHISPERS YOUR NAME

God has given a son to us.... His name will be Wonderful Counselor, Powerful God,...Prince of Peace.

ISAIAH 9:6

*E*very Christmas I read this reminder that came in the mail several years ago: If our greatest need had been information, God would have sent an educator. If our greatest need had been technology, God would have sent us a scientist. If our greatest need had been money, God would have sent us an economist. But since our greatest need was forgiveness, God sent us a Savior.

DECEMBER 15

THE APPLAUSE OF HEAVEN

*Plant goodness, harvest the fruit of loyalty,
plow the new ground of knowledge.*

HOSEA 10:12

*W*ant to see a miracle? Plant a word of love heartdeep in a person's life. Nurture it with a smile and a prayer, and watch what happens. An employee gets a compliment.... A widow is hugged. A gas-station attendant is honored. A preacher is praised. Sowing seeds of peace is like sowing beans. You don't know why it works; you just know it does.... Don't forget the principle. Never underestimate the power of a seed.

JANUARY 18

31 DAYS OF BLESSING

*I ask the Father in his great glory to give you the power
to be strong inwardly through his Spirit.*

EPHESIANS 3:16

It's early morning. Time for young Marcos to leave for school. As he...heads
for the door, he pauses by his father's chair.... Marcos asks, "Blessing, Father?"
The father raises his hand. "God bless you, my son."... Father and child part
for the day, a blessing requested, a blessing willingly given.... We should do the
same. Like the child longing for the father's favor, each of us needs a daily
reminder of our heavenly Father's love.

DECEMBER 14

THE GREAT HOUSE OF GOD

I will be with you always.

MATTHEW 28:20

David said: "I'm asking Yahweh for one thing, only one thing: to live with him in his house my whole life long" (Psalm 27:4 THE MESSAGE)....
What is this house of God which David seeks? When David says, "I will live in the house of the Lord forever" (Psalm 23:6), he's not saying he wants to get away from people. He's saying that he yearns to be in God's presence, wherever he is.

JANUARY 19

WHEN GOD WHISPERS YOUR NAME

I am the good shepherd. I know my sheep, as the Father knows me.
And my sheep know me.

JOHN 10:14

The shepherd knows his sheep. He calls them by name. When we see a crowd,
we see exactly that, a crowd.... We see people, not persons, but people. A herd
of humans. A flock of faces. That's what we see. But not so with the Shepherd.
To him every face is different. Every face is a story. Every face is a child. Every
child has a name.... The shepherd knows his sheep. He knows each one by name.
The Shepherd knows you. He knows your name. And he will never forget it.

DECEMBER 13

WHEN CHRIST COMES

Then wolves will live in peace with lambs,
and leopards will lie down to rest with goats.

ISAIAH 11:6

Can you imagine a world minus sin? Have you done anything recently
because of sin? At the very least, you've complained. You've worried.
You've grumbled. You've hoarded when you should have shared.... Because of sin,
you've snapped at the ones you love and argued with the ones you cherish.
You have felt ashamed, guilty, bitter.... But in heaven, all of this will end. Can you
imagine a world without sin? If so, you can imagine heaven.

JANUARY 20

WHEN CHRIST COMES

To all who did accept him and believe in him he gave the right to become children of God.

JOHN 1:12

While we lived in Rio de Janeiro, we met several American families who came to Brazil to adopt children. They would spend days, sometimes weeks, immersed in a different language and a strange culture. They fought the red tape and paid the large fees, all with the hope of taking a child [home] to the United States.... Hasn't God done the same for us? He entered our culture, battled the resistance, and paid the unspeakable price which adoption required.... We have every legal privilege accorded to [his] child.

DECEMBER 12

JUST LIKE JESUS

We are like clay, and you are the potter;
your hands made us all.

ISAIAH 64:8

*W*here did we get the idea we can't change? From whence come statements
such as, "It's just my nature to worry".... Would we make similar statements
about our bodies? "It's just my nature to have a broken leg. I can't do anything
about it." Of course not. If our bodies malfunction, we seek help. Shouldn't we
do the same with our hearts?... Of course we can. Jesus can change our hearts.
He wants us to have a heart like his.

JANUARY 21

THE GIFT FOR ALL PEOPLE

Surely goodness and mercy shall follow me all the days of my life.
And I will dwell in the house of the Lord forever.

PSALM 23:6 NKJV

*W*hat a surprising way to describe God. A God who pursues us.
Dare we envision a mobile, active God who chases us, tracks us, following
us with goodness and mercy all the days of our lives? He's not hard to find.
He's there in Scripture, looking for Adam and Eve.... Does God wait for them
to come to him? No, the words ring in the garden. "Where are you?" God asks
(Genesis 3:9), beginning his quest to redeem the heart of man.

DECEMBER 11

GOD CAME NEAR

He remembered us when we were in trouble.
His love continues forever.

PSALM 136:23

*G*od chose to reveal himself through a human body. So, people came to him. My, how they came to him! They came at night; they touched him as he walked down the street; they followed him around the sea; they invited him into their homes and placed their children at his feet. Why? Because he refused to be a statue in a cathedral or a priest in an elevated pulpit. He chose instead to be a touchable, approachable, reachable Jesus.

JANUARY 22

WHEN GOD WHISPERS YOUR NAME

Anyone who is having troubles should pray.
Anyone who is happy should sing praises.

JAMES 5:13

Do you want to know how to deepen your prayer life? Pray. Don't prepare to pray.... Don't read about prayer.... Don't attend a lecture on prayer.... Just pray. Posture, tone, and place are personal matters. Select the form that works for you. But don't think about it too much. Don't be so concerned about wrapping the gift that you never give it. Better to pray awkwardly than not at all. And if you feel you should only pray when inspired, that's okay. Just see to it that you are inspired every day.

DECEMBER 10

IN THE GRIP OF GRACE

You prepare a meal for me in front of my enemies.

PSALM 23:5

*P*ause and envision the scene in [God's] royal dining room.... Driven not by our beauty but by his promise, he calls us to himself and invites us to take a permanent place at his table.... We take our place next to the other sinners-made-saints and we share in God's glory.

JANUARY 23

THE APPLAUSE OF HEAVEN

The bride belongs only to the bridegroom.

JOHN 3:29

*J*ohn's descriptions of the future [in the book of Revelation] steals your breath. His depiction of the final battle is graphic…. But in the midst of the battlefield there is a rose…. In this final mountaintop encounter, God pulls back the curtain and allows the warrior to peek into the homeland. When given the task of writing down what he sees, John chooses the most beautiful comparison earth has to offer. The Holy City, John says, is like "a bride beautifully dressed for her husband."

DECEMBER 9

IN THE EYE OF THE STORM

When he arrived, he saw a great crowd waiting. He felt sorry for them.... So he began to teach them many things.

MARK 6:34

When Jesus lands on the shore of Bethsaida, he leaves the Sea of Galilee and steps into a sea of humanity. Keep in mind, he has crossed the sea to get away from the crowds. He needs to grieve. He longs to relax with his followers. He needs anything but another crowd of thousands to teach and heal. But his love for people overcomes his need for rest.

JANUARY 24

IN THE GRIP OF GRACE

*I have learned to be satisfied with the things I have
and with everything that happens.*

PHILIPPIANS 4:11

$\mathcal{T}$est this question: What if God's only gift to you were his grace to save you.
Would you be content? You beg him to save the life of your child. You plead
with him to keep your business afloat. You implore him to remove the cancer
from your body. What if his answer is, "My grace is enough." Would you be
content? You see, from heaven's perspective, grace is enough. If God did
nothing more than save us from hell, could anyone complain?

DECEMBER 8

THE GREAT HOUSE OF GOD

*The Spirit himself bears witness with our Spirit
that we are children of God.*

ROMANS 8:16 NASB

When we come to Christ, God not only forgives us, he also adopts us.... Here is how it happens. You come before the judgment seat of God full of rebellion and mistakes. Because of his justice he cannot dismiss your sin, but because of his love he cannot dismiss you. So, in an act which stunned the heavens, he punished himself on the cross for your sins. God's justice and love are equally honored. And you, God's creation, are forgiven.

JANUARY 25

WALKING WITH THE SAVIOR

When a believing person prays, great things happen.

JAMES 5:16

Prayer is that whole process that reminds us of who God is and who we are. I believe there's great power in prayer. I believe God heals the wounded, and that he can raise the dead. But I don't believe we tell God what to do and when to do it. God knows that we, with our limited vision, don't even know that for which we should pray. When we entrust our requests to him, we trust him to honor our prayers with holy judgment.

DECEMBER 7

HE STILL MOVES STONES

"Lord, don't you care that my sister has left me alone to do all the work?"...
"Martha, Martha, you are worried and upset about many things,"
the Master explained to her. *"Only one thing is important.*
Mary has chosen [it]" (Luke 11:40–42).
What had Mary chosen? She had chosen to sit at the feet of Christ.
God is more pleased with the quiet attention of a sincere servant
than the noisy service of a sour one.... What matters more than the
type of service is the heart behind the service.

JANUARY 26

WHEN CHRIST COMES

God will wipe away every tear from their eyes, and there will be no more death, sadness, crying, or pain.

REVELATION 21:4

What have you done today to avoid death? Likely a lot.... Why? Why the effort? Because you are worried about staying alive. That won't be a worry in heaven.... We are not made of steel, we are made of dust. And this life is not crowned with life, it is crowned with death. The next life, however, is different. Jesus urged the Christians in Smyrna to "be faithful, even if you have to die, and I will give you the crown of life" (Revelation 2:10).

DECEMBER 6

IN THE GRIP OF GRACE

Nothing...in the whole world will ever be able to separate us from the love of God.

ROMANS 8:39

*C*an anything separate us from the love Christ has for us? God answered our question before we asked it. So we'd see his answer, he lit the sky with a star. So we'd hear it, he filled the night with a choir; and so we'd believe it, he did what no man had ever dreamed. He became flesh and dwelt among us. He placed his hand on the shoulder of humanity and said, "You're something special."

JANUARY 27

HE STILL MOVES STONES

I will be your father, and you will be my sons and daughters,
says the Lord Almighty.

2 CORINTHIANS 6:18

$\mathcal{W}$e can't control the way our family responds to us. When it comes to the behavior of others toward us, our hands are tied. We have to move beyond the naive expectation that if we do good, people will treat us right. The fact is they may and they may not.... Let God give you what your family doesn't. If your earthly father doesn't affirm you, then let your heavenly Father take his place.... [And] don't lose heart. God still changes families.

DECEMBER 5

HE STILL MOVES STONES

*Daughter, your faith has made you well. Go in peace,
and be healed of your affliction.*

MARK 5:34 NKJV

*M*aybe all you have [is] a crazy hunch and a high hope. You have nothing
to give. But you are hurting. And all you have to offer him is your hurt. If that
describes you, note carefully,...one person [whom Christ] commended...for
having faith...was a shame-struck, penniless outcast—[a woman who had been
bleeding for twelve years]—who clutched onto her hunch that he could and her
hope that he would. Which, by the way, isn't a bad definition of faith.

JANUARY 28

THE GREAT HOUSE OF GOD

Lord you have done such great things!
How deep are your thoughts!

PSALM 92:5

God's thoughts are not our thoughts, nor are they even like ours.... "I'm going to live before I die," we resolve. "Die, so you can live," he instructs. We love what rusts. He loves what endures. We rejoice at our successes. He rejoices at our confessions. We show our children the Nike star with the million-dollar smile and say, "Be like Mike." God points to the crucified carpenter with bloody lips and a torn side and says, "Be like Christ."

DECEMBER 4

JUST LIKE JESUS

*The wisdom that comes from God is first of all pure,
then peaceful, gentle, and easy to please.*

JAMES 3:17

The heart of Jesus was pure. The Savior was adored by thousands, yet content
to live a simple life.... Jesus' heart was peaceful. The disciples fretted over the
need to feed the thousands, but not Jesus. He thanked God for the problem.
The disciples shouted for fear in the storm, but not Jesus. He slept through it.
Peter drew his sword to fight the soldiers, but not Jesus. He lifted his hand
to heal. His heart was at peace.

JANUARY 29

IN THE GRIP OF GRACE

When people sin, they earn what sin pays—death.

ROMANS 6:23

Sin does to a life what shears do to a flower. A cut at the stem separates
a flower from the source of life…. A dead soul has no life. Cut off from God,
the soul withers and dies. The consequence of sin is not a bad day or a bad mood
but a dead soul. The sign of a dead soul is clear: poisoned lips and cursing
mouths, feet that lead to violence and eyes that don't see God…. The finished
work of sin is to kill the soul.

DECEMBER 3

IN THE EYE OF THE STORM

He had compassion on them.

MATTHEW 14:14 NIV

The Greek word for compassion is *splanchnizomai*.... "Splanchnology" is a study of...the gut. When Matthew writes that Jesus had compassion on the people, he is not saying that Jesus felt casual pity for them.... Matthew is saying that Jesus felt their hurt in his gut: He felt the limp of the crippled. He felt the hurt of the diseased. He felt the loneliness of the leper. He felt the embarrassment of the sinful. And once he felt their hurts, he couldn't help but heal their hurts.

JANUARY 30

HE STILL MOVES STONES

The ways of God are without fault.

PSALM 18:30

When God doesn't do what we want, it's not easy. Never has been. Never will be. But faith is the conviction that God knows more than we do about this life and He will get us through it. Remember, disappointment is cured by revamped expectations.

DECEMBER 2

THE GREAT HOUSE OF GOD

God's peace, which is so great we cannot understand it,
will keep your hearts and minds in Christ Jesus.

PHILIPPIANS 4:7

The Lord came to Gideon and told him he was to lead his people in victory over the Midianites. That's like God telling a housewife to stand up to her abusive husband or a high school student to take on drug peddlers.... "Y-y-you-b-b-better get somebody else," we stammer. But then God reminds us that he knows we can't, but he can, and to prove it he gives a wonderful gift. He brings a spirit of peace.

JANUARY 31

IN THE GRIP OF GRACE

He will rejoice over you. You will rest in his love;
he will sing and be joyful about you.

ZEPHANIAH 3:17

God is for you. Turn to the sidelines; that's God cheering your run. Look past the finish line; that's God applauding your steps. Listen for him in the bleachers, shouting your name. Too tired to continue? He'll carry you. Too discouraged to fight? He's picking you up. God is for you. God is for you. Had he a calendar, your birthday would be circled. If he drove a car, your name would be on his bumper. If there's a tree in heaven, he's carved your name in the bark.

DECEMBER 1

JUST LIKE JESUS

People harvest only what they plant.
GALATIANS 6:7

$\mathscr{T}$hink for a moment of your heart as a greenhouse.... And your heart, like a greenhouse, has to be managed. Consider for a moment your thoughts as seed. Some thoughts become flowers. Others become weeds.... Ever wonder why some people have the Teflon capacity to resist negativism and remain patient, optimistic, and forgiving? Could it be that they have diligently sown seeds of goodness and are enjoying the harvest?

FEBRUARY 1

WHEN CHRIST COMES

The Lord will reward everyone for whatever good he does,
whether he is slave or free.

EPHESIANS 6:8 NIV

For all we don't know about the next life, this much is certain: The day Christ comes will be a day of reward. Those who went unknown on earth will be known in heaven. Those who never heard the cheers of men will hear the cheers of angels. Those who missed the blessing of a father will hear the blessing of their heavenly Father. The small will be great. The forgotten will be remembered. The unnoticed will be crowned and the faithful will be honored.

NOVEMBER 30

WHEN CHRIST COMES

The Word became human and lived here on earth among us.
He was full of unfailing love and faithfulness.

JOHN 1:14 NLT

*T*he operative word of the verse is *among*. He lived among us.
He donned the costliest of robes: a human body. He made a throne out
of a manger and a royal court out of some cows. He took a common name—
Jesus—and made it holy. He took common people and made them the same.
He could have lived over us or away from us. But he didn't.
He lived among us.

FEBRUARY 2

IN THE GRIP OF GRACE

I pray that you...will have the power to understand the greatness of Christ's love—how wide and how long and how high and how deep that love is.

EPHESIANS 3:18

There is no way our little minds can comprehend the love of God. But that didn't keep him from coming.... From the cradle in Bethlehem to the cross in Jerusalem we've pondered the love of our Father. What can you say to that kind of emotion? Upon learning that God would rather die than live without you, how do you react? How can you begin to explain such passion?

NOVEMBER 29

WHEN CHRIST COMES

Hold on to what you have, so that no one will take your crown.

REVELATION 3:11 NIV

Some of you have never won a prize in your life. All you have are "almosts" and "what ifs." If that hits home, then you'll cherish this promise: "And when the Chief Shepherd appears, you will receive the crown of glory that will never fade away" (1 Peter 5:4 NIV).

Your day is coming. What the world has overlooked, your Father has remembered, and sooner than you can imagine, you will be blessed by him.

FEBRUARY 3

WALKING WITH THE SAVIOR

Praise the Lord, God our Savior, who helps us every day.

PSALM 68:19

Christ will not turn away from you. He came first and foremost to those who have no hope. He goes to those no one else would go to and says, "I'll give you eternity." Only you can surrender your concerns to the Father. No one else can take those away and give them to God. Only you can cast all your anxieties on the one who cares for you. What better way to start the day than by laying your cares at his feet?

NOVEMBER 28

HE STILL MOVES STONES

The Lord is close to everyone who prays to him,
to all who truly pray to him.

PSALM 145:18

Healing begins when we do something. Healing begins when we
reach out. Healing starts when we take a step. God's help is near
and always available, but it is only given to those who seek it. Nothing
results from apathy.... God honors radical, risk-taking faith.
When arks are built, lives are saved. When soldiers march,
Jerichos tumble. When staffs are raised, seas still open.
When a lunch is shared, thousands are fed.

FEBRUARY 4

JUST LIKE JESUS

I have obeyed my Father's commands, and I remain in his love. In the same way, if you obey my commands, you will remain in my love.

JOHN 15:10

God rewards those who seek him.... Can you think of a greater gift than to be like Jesus? Christ felt no guilt; God wants to banish yours. Jesus had no bad habits; God wants to remove yours. Jesus had no fear of death; God wants you to be fearless. Jesus had kindness for the diseased and mercy for the rebellious and courage for the challenges. God wants you to have the same....

He wants you to be just like Jesus.

NOVEMBER 27

JUST LIKE JESUS

*He came to serve others and to give his life as a ransom
for many people.*

MATTHEW 20:28

Jesus aimed at one goal—to save humanity from its sin.... Jesus was so
focused on his task that he knew when to say, "It is finished" (John 19:30).
But he was not so focused on his goal that he was unpleasant. Quite the
contrary. How pleasant were his thoughts! Children couldn't resist Jesus.
He could find beauty in lilies, joy in worship, and possibilities in problems.

FEBRUARY 5

A GENTLE THUNDER

The Lord is my shepherd; I have everything I need.

PSALM 23:1

Sheep aren't smart. They tend to wander into running creeks for water, then their wool grows heavy and they drown. They need a shepherd to lead them to "calm water." They have no natural defense—no claws, no horns, no fangs.... Sheep need a shepherd with a "rod..." to protect them. They have no sense of direction. They need someone to lead them "on paths that are right." So do we.... We need a shepherd to care for us and to guide us. And we have one. One who knows us by name.

NOVEMBER 26

THE GREAT HOUSE OF GOD

God can do all things.

MARK 10:27

*O*ur questions betray our lack of understanding: How can God hear
all the prayers which come to him? (Perhaps his ears are different from yours.)
If people down here won't forgive me, how much more am I guilty before a
holy God? (Oh, just the opposite. God is always able to give grace
when we humans can't—he invented it.)

FEBRUARY 6

IN THE GRIP OF GRACE

I said, "I will confess my sins to the Lord,"
and you forgave my guilt.

PSALM 32:5

Once there were a couple of farmers who couldn't get along with each other. A wide ravine separated their two farms...[and] each constructed a fence... to keep the other out. In time, however, the daughter of one met the son of the other, and the couple fell in love. Determined not to be kept apart...they tore down the fence and used the wood to build a bridge across the ravine. Confession does that. Confessed sin becomes the bridge over which we can walk back into the presence of God.

NOVEMBER 25

THE GREAT HOUSE OF GOD

*I'm asking Yahweh for one thing, only one thing: to live
with him in his house my whole life long. I'll contemplate
his beauty, I'll study at his feet. That's the only quiet
secure place in a noisy world.*

PSALM 27:4-5 THE MESSAGE

If you could ask God for one thing, what would you request? David tells
us...[he] longs to live in the house of God. I emphasize the word *live*....
He doesn't ask for a meal or to spend an evening in God's house.
He wants to move in with him...forever.

FEBRUARY 7

WHEN CHRIST COMES

*When the master comes and finds the servant doing his work,
the servant will be blessed.*

MATTHEW 24:46

For every million who aspire, only one achieves. The vast majority of us don't hit the big ball, don't feel the ticker tape, don't wear the gold medal, don't give the valedictory address. And that's OK. We understand that in the economy of earth, there are a limited number of crowns. The economy of heaven, however, is refreshingly different. Heavenly rewards are not limited to a chosen few, but "to all those who have waited with love for him to come again" (2 Timothy 4:8).

NOVEMBER 24

IN THE EYE OF THE STORM

He took our suffering on him and felt our pain for us.

ISAIAH 53:4

*J*esus knows how you feel. You are precious to him. So precious that he became like you so that you would come to him. When you struggle, he listens. When you yearn, he responds. When you question, he hears. He has been there.

FEBRUARY 8

HE STILL MOVES STONES

My true brother and sister and mother are those who do what God wants.

MARK 3:35

*D*oes Jesus have anything to say about dealing with difficult relatives?... You may not be aware that Jesus had brothers and sisters (see Mark 6:3).... And it may surprise you to know that his family was less than perfect.... [Yet] he didn't try to control his family's behavior, nor did he let their behavior control his. He didn't demand that they agree with him. He didn't sulk when they insulted him. He didn't make it his mission to try to please them.

NOVEMBER 23

THE INSPIRATIONAL STUDY BIBLE

Rejoice in the Lord always. Again I will say, rejoice!

PHILIPPIANS 4:4

Let's go to Rome...to a rather drab little room, surrounded by high walls.... Inside we see a man seated on the floor.... It is the apostle Paul.... The apostle who was bound only by the will of God is now in chains.... He is writing a letter. No doubt it is a complaint letter to God.... But he doesn't [complain]. Instead, he writes a letter that two thousand years later is still known as the treatise on joy—Philippians.... Why don't you spend some time with it?

FEBRUARY 9

THE APPLAUSE OF HEAVEN

In Christ Jesus, God made us to do good works, which God planned in advance for us to live our lives doing.

EPHESIANS 2:10

$\mathcal{T}$he desire for excellence is a gift of God, much needed in society. It is characterized by respect for quality and a yearning to use God's gifts in a way that pleases him.... But there is a canyon of difference between doing your best to glorify God and doing whatever it takes to glorify yourself. The quest for excellence is a mark of maturity. The quest for power is childish.

NOVEMBER 22

IN THE GRIP OF GRACE

As far as the east is from the west, so far has He removed our transgressions from us.

PSALM 103:12

Confession does for the soul what preparing the land does for the field. Before the farmer sows the seed he works the acreage, removing the rocks and pulling the stumps. He knows that seed grows better if the land is prepared. Confession is the act of inviting God to walk the acreage of our hearts.... And so the Father and the Son walk the field together; digging and pulling, preparing the heart for fruit.

FEBRUARY 10

IN THE GRIP OF GRACE

Whoever comes to me will never be hungry,
and whoever believes in me will never be thirsty.

JOHN 6:35

*T*here are times when the one thing you want is the one thing you never get....
May I ask a very important question? What if God says no? What if the request
is delayed or even denied? When God says no to you, how will you respond?
If God says, "I've given you my grace, and that is enough," will you be content?
Content. That's the word. A state of heart in which you would be at peace
if God gave you nothing more than he already has.

NOVEMBER 21

HE STILL MOVES STONES

Suppose someone...sees a brother or sister in need,
but does not help. Then God's love is not living in that person.

1 JOHN 3:17

$\mathcal{L}$eo Tolstoy tells of the time he...passed a beggar. Tolstoy reached into his pocket to give the beggar some money, but his pocket was empty. Tolstoy... said, "I'm sorry, my brother, but I have nothing to give." The beggar brightened and said, "You have given me more than I asked for—you have called me brother." To the love-starved, a word of affection can be a feast.

FEBRUARY 11

JUST LIKE JESUS

He is a rewarder of them that diligently seek him.

HEBREWS 11:6 KJV

*D*iligently—what a great word. Be diligent in your search. Be hungry in your quest, relentless in your pilgrimage.... Step away from the puny pursuits of possessions and positions, and seek your king. Don't be satisfied with angels. Don't be content with stars in the sky. Seek him out as the shepherds did. Long for him as Simeon did. Worship him as the wise men did. Do as John and Andrew did: ask for his address. Do as Matthew: invite Jesus into your house. Imitate Zacchaeus. Risk whatever it takes to see Christ.

NOVEMBER 20

THE GREAT HOUSE OF GOD

The heavens tell the glory of God.

PSALM 19:1

*H*ow vital that we pray, armed with the knowledge that God is in heaven....
Spend some time walking in the workshop of the heavens, seeing what God has
done, and watch how your prayers are energized.... Hold a dime in your fingers
and extend it arm's length toward the sky...and you will block out fifteen million
stars from your view.... By showing us the heavens, Jesus is showing us his
Father's workshop.... He taps us on the shoulder and says, "Your Father
can handle that for you."

FEBRUARY 12

WALKING WITH THE SAVIOR

If we live, we are living for the Lord, and if we die,
we are dying for the Lord.

ROMANS 14:8

*D*o you wonder where you can go for encouragement and motivation?
Go back to that moment when you first saw the love of Jesus Christ....
Run to Jesus. Jesus wants you to go to him. He wants to become the most
important person in your life, the greatest love you'll ever know. He wants
you to love him so much that there's no room in your heart and in your
life for sin. Invite him to take up residence in your heart.

NOVEMBER 19

HE STILL MOVES STONES

Those who try to keep their lives will lose them.
But those who give up their lives will save them.

LUKE 17:33

There is a rawness and a wonder to life. Pursue it. Hunt for it. Sell out to get
it.... Your goal is not to live long; it's to live. Jesus says the options are clear.
On one side there is the voice of safety.... Or you can hear the voice
of adventure—God's adventure. Instead of building a fire in your hearth,
build a fire in your heart. Follow God's impulses.... Make a difference.

FEBRUARY 13

A GENTLE THUNDER

If we are not faithful, he will still be faithful,
because he cannot be false to himself.

2 TIMOTHY 2:13

God's blessings are dispensed according to the riches of his grace, not according to the depth of our faith.... Why is that important to know? So you won't get cynical.... So what do we do? Throw up our hands and walk away? Tell the world we can't help them? No, we don't give up. We look up. We trust. We believe. And our optimism is not hollow. Christ has proven worthy. He has shown that he never fails. That's what makes God, God.

NOVEMBER 18

WHEN CHRIST COMES

God will praise each one of them.

1 CORINTHIANS 4:5

*W*hat an incredible sentence.... Not "the best of them" nor "a few of them" nor "the achievers among them," but "God will praise each one of them." You won't be left out. God will see to that. In fact, God himself will give the praise.... And what's more, the praise is personal!... The crowns are given one at a time. God himself will look you in the eye and bless you with the words, "Well done, good and faithful servant!" (Matthew 25:23 NIV).

FEBRUARY 14

A GENTLE THUNDER

If people want to follow me, they must give up the things they want. They must be willing even to give up their lives to follow me.

MARK 8:34

On one side stands the crowd. Jeering. Baiting. Demanding. On the other stands a peasant. Swollen lips. Lumpy eye. Lofty promise. One promises acceptance, the other a cross. One offers flesh and flash, the other offers faith. The crowd challenges, "Follow us and fit in." Jesus promises, "Follow me and stand out." They promise to please. God promises to save. God looks at you and asks, "Which will be your choice?"

NOVEMBER 17

JUST LIKE JESUS

The Son does whatever the Father does.

JOHN 5:19

The crowning attribute of Christ was this: his heart was spiritual. His thoughts reflected his intimate relationship with the Father.... Jesus took his instructions from God. It was his habit to go to worship. It was his practice to memorize Scripture.... His times of prayer guided him. He once returned from prayer and announced it was time to move to another city. Another time of prayer resulted in the selection of the disciples. Jesus was led by an unseen hand.... The heart of Jesus was spiritual.

FEBRUARY 15

WHEN GOD WHISPERS YOUR NAME

Now we do not live following our sinful selves,
but we live following the Spirit.

ROMANS 8:4

*T*hink about this. Spiritual life comes from the Spirit! Your parents may
have given you genes, but God gives you grace. Your parents may be responsible
for your body, but God has taken charge of your soul. You may get your looks
from your mother, but you get eternity from your Father, your heavenly Father.
And God is willing to give you what your family didn't.

NOVEMBER 16

THE APPLAUSE OF HEAVEN

Those people who know they have great spiritual needs are happy, because the kingdom of heaven belongs to them.

MATTHEW 5:3

[God] promises [sacred delight]. And he promises it to an
unlikely crowd: The poor in spirit, those who mourn, the merciful,
the pure in heart, the peacemakers, the persecuted.
It is to this band of pilgrims that God promises a special
blessing. A heavenly joy. A sacred delight.

FEBRUARY 16

WALKING WITH THE SAVIOR

If any of you needs wisdom, you should ask God for it.

JAMES 1:5

Thomas came with doubts. Did Christ turn him away? Moses had his reservations. Did God tell him to go home? Job had his struggles. Did God avoid him? Paul had his hard times. Did God abandon him? No. God never turns away the sincere heart. Tough questions don't stump God. He invites our probing. Mark it down. God never turns away the honest seeker. Go to God with your questions. You may not find all the answers, but in finding God, you know the One who does.

NOVEMBER 15

GOD CAME NEAR

I did this as an example so that you should do as I have done for you.

JOHN 13:15

We are what we see.... Humans were never meant to dwell in the stale fog of the lowlands with no vision of their Creator.... Seeing Jesus is what Christianity is all about. Christian service, in its purest form, is nothing more than imitating him whom we see. To see his majesty and to imitate him, that is the sum of Christianity.

FEBRUARY 17

JUST LIKE JESUS

*May he enlighten the eyes of your mind so that you can see
what hope his call holds for you.*

EPHESIANS 1:18 NIV

The world has never known a heart so pure, a character so flawless.
His spiritual hearing was so keen he never missed a heavenly whisper.
His mercy so abundant he never missed a chance to forgive.... Jesus is the
ultimate model for every person.... God urges you to fix your eyes upon Jesus.
Heaven invites you to set the lens of your heart on the heart of the Savior
and make him the object of your life.

NOVEMBER 14

THE GREAT HOUSE OF GOD

Look at the birds in the air. They don't plant or harvest or store food in barns, but your heavenly Father feeds them.

MATTHEW 6:26

It [God] is able to place the stars in their sockets and suspend the sky like a curtain, do you think it is remotely possible that God is able to guide your life?... If he cares enough about the planet Saturn to give it rings or Venus to make it sparkle, is there an outside chance that he cares enough about you to meet your needs?

FEBRUARY 18

HE STILL MOVES STONES

*Do not lose the courage you had in the past, which has
a great reward.*

HEBREWS 10:35

*A*re you a bruised reed? Was it so long ago that you stood so tall, so proud?...
Then something happened.... The world will break you off; the world will snuff
you out. But the artists of Scripture proclaim that God won't. Painted on canvas
after canvas is the tender touch of a Creator who has a special place for the
bruised and weary of the world. A God who is the friend of the wounded heart.

NOVEMBER 13

WHEN GOD WHISPERS YOUR NAME

So let us go on to grown-up teaching. Let us not go back
over the beginning lessons we learned about Christ.

HEBREWS 6:1

Pick a time in the not-too-distant past. A year or two ago. Now ask
yourself a few questions. How does your prayer life today compare with then?
How about your giving? Have both the amount and the joy increased?
What about your church loyalty? Can you tell you've grown?
And Bible study? Are you learning to learn?

FEBRUARY 19

IN THE EYE OF THE STORM

Thank the Lord because he is good. His love continues forever.

PSALM 106:1

*W*orship is when you're aware that what you've been given is far greater than what you can give.... Worship is the "thank you" that refuses to be silenced. We have tried to make a science out of worship. We can't do that. We can't do that any more than we can "sell love" or "negotiate peace." Worship is a voluntary act of gratitude offered by the saved to the Savior, by the healed to the Healer, and by the delivered to the Deliverer.

NOVEMBER 12

HE STILL MOVES STONES

We all know that God does not listen to sinners,
but he listens to anyone who worships and obeys him.

JOHN 9:31

Most of our prayer lives could use a tune-up. Some prayer lives lack
consistency.... Others of us need sincerity.... Still others lack, well, honesty.
We honestly wonder if prayer makes a difference.... Our prayers may be
awkward. Our attempts may be feeble. But since the power of prayer is
in the one who hears it and not the one who says it, our prayers
do make a difference.

FEBRUARY 20

IN THE GRIP OF GRACE

If you hide your sins, you will not succeed.

PROVERBS 28:13

$\mathcal{O}$ur baseball coach had a firm rule against chewing tobacco.... [But] before long we'd all tried it.... One day I'd just popped a plug in my mouth when one of the players warned, "Here comes the coach!" Not wanting to get caught... I swallowed. Gulp.... I paid the price for hiding my disobedience. My body was not made to ingest tobacco. Your soul was not made to ingest sin.... Are you keeping any secrets from God?... Take a pointer from a nauseated third baseman. You'll feel better if you get it out.

NOVEMBER 11

WHEN GOD WHISPERS YOUR NAME

There are many rooms in my Father's house;...I am going there to prepare a place for you.

JOHN 14:2

Try this. Imagine a perfect world. Whatever that means to you, imagine it. Does that mean peace? Then envision absolute tranquility. Does a perfect world imply joy? Then create your highest happiness. Will a perfect world have love? If so, ponder a place where love has no bounds. Whatever heaven means to you, imagine it.... And then smile as the Father reminds you, No one has ever imagined what God has prepared for those who love him.

FEBRUARY 21

WHEN CHRIST COMES

*They have washed their robes and made them white
in the blood of the Lamb.*

REVELATION 7:14

God has only one requirement for entrance into heaven: that we be clothed
in Christ.... The inhabitants of heaven...are dressed in white. The saints.
The elders.... How would you suppose Jesus is dressed? In white?... "He is dressed
in a robe dipped in blood, and his name is the Word of God" (Revelation 19:13).
Why is Christ's robe not white?... Paul says simply, "He changed places with us"
(Galatians 3:13).... He wore our coat of sin to the cross.

NOVEMBER 10

JUST LIKE JESUS

*We Christians actually do have within us a portion
of the very thoughts and mind of Christ.*

1 CORINTHIANS 2:16 TLB

*H*ow could we ever hope to have the heart of Jesus? Ready for a surprise?
You already do.... If you are in Christ, you already have the heart of Christ....
He has made your heart his home.... He has moved in and unpacked his
bags and is ready to change you "into his likeness from one degree of glory
to another" (2 Corinthians 3:18 RSV).

FEBRUARY 22

HE STILL MOVES STONES

Jesus said [to her], "I also don't judge you guilty. You may go now, but don't sin anymore."

JOHN 8:11

*I*nvite Christ to journey with you...to stand beside you as you retell the events of the darkest nights of your soul. And then listen. Listen carefully. He's speaking.... "I don't judge you guilty." And watch. Watch carefully. He's writing. He's leaving a message. Not in the sand, but on a cross. Not with his hand, but with his blood. His message has two words: Not guilty.

NOVEMBER 9

HE STILL MOVES STONES

*Faith means being sure of the things we hope for and knowing
that something is real even if we do not see it.*

HEBREWS 11:1

Faith is the belief that God is real and that God is good.... It is a choice
to believe that the one who made it all hasn't left it all and that he still sends
light into the shadows.... God says that the more hopeless your circumstances,
the more likely, your salvation.... God's help is near and always available,
but it is only given to those who seek it.

FEBRUARY 23

THE APPLAUSE OF HEAVEN

*He comforts us every time we have trouble, so when others
have trouble, we can comfort them.*

2 CORINTHIANS 1:4

I'm not a hero.... I'm a parent. When a child hurts, a parent does what comes
naturally. He helps.... Why don't I let my Father do for me what I am more than
willing to do for my own children? I'm learning.... Being a father is teaching
me...there is a Father who will hold me until I'm better, help me until I can live
with the hurt, and who won't go to sleep when I'm afraid of waking up
and seeing the dark. Ever.

NOVEMBER 8

THE GREAT HOUSE OF GOD

Be still, and know that I am God.

PSALM 46:10 NIV

The word holy means "to separate." The ancestry of the term can be traced back to an ancient word which means "to cut." To be holy, then, is to be a cut above the norm, superior, extraordinary.... The Holy One dwells on a different level from the rest of us. What frightens us does not frighten him. What troubles us does not trouble him.... When you set your sights on our God, you focus on one "a cut above" any storm life may bring.... You find peace.

FEBRUARY 24

JUST LIKE JESUS

Think about Jesus' example. He held on while wicked people were doing evil things to him. So do not get tired and stop trying.

HEBREWS 12:3

Jesus...is the only person to live on earth after he had lived in heaven. As believers, you and I will live in heaven after time on earth, but Jesus did just the opposite.... And knowing what awaited him in heaven enabled him to bear the shame on earth.... In his final moments, Jesus focused on the joy God put before him.... By focusing on the prize, he was able not only to finish the race but to finish it strong.

NOVEMBER 7

A GENTLE THUNDER

Nathanael said to Philip, "Can anything good come from Nazareth?" Philip answered, "Come and see."

JOHN 1:46

*N*athanael's question still lingers, even two thousand years later.... Can anything good come out of Nazareth? Come and see. Come and see the pierced hand of God touch the most common heart, wipe the tear from the wrinkled face, and forgive the ugliest sin. Come and see. He avoids no seeker. He ignores no probe. He fears no search. Come and see.

FEBRUARY 25

IN THE GRIP OF GRACE

We love because God first loved us.

1 JOHN 4:19

*U*ntethered by time, he sees us all.... From the hut-builders
to the finger-pointers to the rock-stackers, he sees us. Vagabonds
and ragamuffins all, he saw us before we were born.
And he loves what he sees. Flooded by emotion. Overcome by pride,
the Starmaker turns to us, one by one, and says, "You are my child.
I love you dearly. I'm aware that someday you'll turn from me and walk away.
But I want you to know, I've already provided you a way back."

NOVEMBER 6

IN THE EYE OF THE STORM

The rich and the poor are alike in that the Lord made them all.

PROVERBS 22:2

*H*ave you noticed that God doesn't ask you to prove that you will put your salary to good use? Have you noticed that God doesn't turn off your oxygen supply when you misuse his gifts? Aren't you glad that God doesn't give you only that which you remember to thank him for?... God's goodness is spurred by his nature, not by our worthiness.

FEBRUARY 26

THE GREAT HOUSE OF GOD

Lord, I love the Temple where you live, where your glory is.

PSALM 26:8

*W*hen it comes to resting your soul, there is no place like the
Great House of God.

NOVEMBER 5

HE STILL MOVES STONES

When you were spiritually dead because of your sins and because you were not free from the power of your sinful self, God made you alive with Christ, and he forgave all our sins. He canceled the debt.... With the cross, he won the victory and showed the world that they were powerless.

COLOSSIAN 2:13-15

*A*s you look at the words above, answer this question. Who is doing the work? You or God? Who is active? You or God? Who is doing the saving? You or God?

FEBRUARY 27

IN THE GRIP OF GRACE

I look at your heavens, which you made with your fingers....
But why are people important to you?

PSALM 8:3-4

The loss of mystery has led to the loss of majesty. The more we know, the less we believe. Strange, don't you think? Knowledge of the workings shouldn't negate wonder. Knowledge should stir wonder. Who has more reason to worship than the astronomer who has seen the stars?... We are more impressed with our discovery of the light switch than with the one who invented electricity.... Rather than worship the Creator, we worship the creation.

NOVEMBER 4

IN THE GRIP OF GRACE

Their thinking became useless. Their foolish minds were filled with darkness. They said they were wise, but they became fools.

ROMANS 1:21-22

Since the hedonist has never seen the hand who made the universe, he assumes there is no life beyond the here and now.... No purpose beyond his own pleasure. No divine factor.... His life is so desperate for pleasure that he has no time or room for God. Is he right?... Paul says, "Absolutely not!"...we lose more than stained-glass windows when we dismiss God. We lose our standard, our purpose, and our worship.

FEBRUARY 28

JUST LIKE JESUS

Let us run the race that is before us and never give up.

HEBREWS 12:1

The word race is from the Greek agon, from which we get the word agony. The Christian's race is not a jog but rather a demanding and grueling, sometimes agonizing race. It takes a massive effort to finish strong.... By contrast, Jesus' best work was his final work, and his strongest step was his last step. Our Master is the classic example of one who endured.... He could have quit the race. But he didn't.

NOVEMBER 3

IN THE GRIP OF GRACE

*Can a mother forget the baby at her breast and have
no compassion on the child she has borne?*

ISAIAH 49:15 NIV

*W*hat a bizarre question. Can you mothers imagine feeding your infant
and then later asking, "What was that baby's name?" No. I've seen you care
for your young. You stroke the hair, you touch the face, you sing the name
over and over. Can a mother forget? No way. But "even if she could forget,...
I will not forget you," God pledges (Isaiah 49:15).

FEBRUARY 29

A GENTLE THUNDER

Everyone who asks will receive. Everyone who searches will find.
MATTHEW 7:8

*O*nce there was a man who dared God to speak: Burn the bush like you did
for Moses.... Collapse the walls like you did for Joshua.... Still the waves like you
did on Galilee, God. And I will listen. And so the man...waited for God to speak.
And God heard the man, so God answered. He sent fire...for a church.
He brought down a wall...of sin. He stilled a storm...of a soul.... But because
the man was looking at bushes...bricks and...seas, he...asked, Have you lost
your power? And God...said, Have you lost your hearing?

NOVEMBER 2

WHEN CHRIST COMES

*No one has ever imagined what God has prepared
for those who love him.*

1 CORINTHIANS 2:9

*T*hink about the day Christ comes.... Though you are one of a throng,
it's as if you and Jesus are all alone.... I wonder if Christ might say these words
to you: "I'm so proud that you let me use you. Because of you, others are here
today. Would you like to meet them?"... One by one, they begin to step out....
It's not long before you and your Savior are encircled by the delightful
collection of souls you've touched.

MARCH 1

IN THE GRIP OF GRACE

Then you will know the truth, and the truth will make you free.

JOHN 8:32

Sin put you in prison.... Then Jesus came and paid your bail. He served your time; he satisfied the penalty, and set you free. Christ died, and when you cast your lot with him, your old self died too. The only way to be set free from the prison of sin is to serve its penalty. In this case the penalty is death. Someone has to die, either you or a heaven-sent substitute.... And when Jesus died, you died to sin's claim on your life. You are free.

NOVEMBER 1

A GENTLE THUNDER

You should be a light for other people. Live so that they will see the good things you do and will praise your Father in heaven.

MATTHEW 5:16

You want to make a difference in your world? Live a holy life: Be faithful to your spouse.... Be the neighbor who acts neighborly. Be the employee who does the work and doesn't complain. Pay your bills. Do your part and enjoy life. Don't speak one message and live another. People are watching the way we act more than they are listening to what we say.

MARCH 2

HE STILL MOVES STONES

In all these things we have full victory through God who showed his love for us.

ROMANS 8:37

When it comes to healing our spiritual condition, we don't have a chance.... Our only hope is that God will...step out of the temple and step into our ward of hurt and helplessness. Which is exactly what he has done.... I wish we would take Jesus at his word.... When he says we're forgiven, let's unload the guilt. When he says we're valuable, let's believe him.... When he says we're provided for, let's stop worrying. God's efforts are strongest when our efforts are useless.

OCTOBER 31

THE GREAT HOUSE OF GOD

Let us, then, feel very sure that we can come before God's throne where there is grace.

HEBREWS 4:16

$\mathcal{W}$hen you [pray], "Thy kingdom come," you are inviting the Messiah himself to walk into your world. "Come, my King!... Be present in my heart.... Come into my marriage. Be Lord of my family, my fears, and my doubts." This is no feeble request; it's a bold appeal for God to occupy every corner of your life. Who are you to ask such a thing?... You are his child, for heaven's sake! And so you ask boldly.

MARCH 3

WHEN CHRIST COMES

After I go and prepare a place for you, I will come back and take
you to be with me so that you may be where I am.

JOHN 14:3

Someday, according to Christ, he will set us free. He will come back.
In the blink of an eye, as fast as the lightning flashes..., he will come back.
And everyone will see him—you will, I will. Bodies will push back the dirt
and break the surface of the sea. The earth will tremble, the sky will roar,
and those who do not know him will shudder. But...you will not fear,
because you know him.

OCTOBER 30

JUST LIKE JESUS

Who is more important: the one sitting at the table or the one serving? You think the one at the table is more important, but I am like a servant among you.

LUKE 22:27

*I*n Jesus' day the washing of feet was a task reserved not just for servants but for the lowest of servants.... [But] in this case the one with the towel and basin is the king of the universe.... Hours before his own death, Jesus' concern is singular. He wants his disciples to know how much he loves them. More than removing dirt, Jesus is removing doubt.

MARCH 4

IN THE EYE OF THE STORM

We know the love that God has for us, and we trust that love.

1 JOHN 4:16

You can't take the wet out of water and still have water. You can't take the heat out of fire and still have fire. In the same way, you can't take the love out of [God]...and still have him exist. For he was...and is...Love. Probe deep within him. Explore every corner. Search every angle. Love is all you find. Go to the beginning of every decision he has made and you'll find it. Go to the end of every story he has told and you'll see it. Love.

OCTOBER 29

THE APPLAUSE OF HEAVEN

*Come to me, all of you who are tired and have heavy loads,
and I will give you rest.*

MATTHEW 11:28

*A*s long as Jesus is one of many options, he is no option....
And as long as you can take him or leave him, you might as well
leave him, because he won't be taken half-heartedly.
But when you...admit that you have no other option..., and when there
is truly no other name that you can call, then cast all your cares on him,
for he is waiting in the midst of the storm.

MARCH 5

THE GREAT HOUSE OF GOD

I have good plans for you, not plans to hurt you.

JEREMIAH 29:11

*L*ast night during family devotions...I placed a collection of food [on the table]: some fruit, some raw vegetables, and some Oreo cookies. "Every day," I explained, "God prepares for us a plate of experiences. What kind of plate do you most enjoy?"... Some days are "three-cookie days." Many are not.... Apparently God knows we need some strength, and though the portion may be hard to swallow, isn't it for our own good?... And the next time your plate has a portion you find hard to swallow, talk to God about it. Jesus did.

OCTOBER 28

THE APPLAUSE OF HEAVEN

Jesus was "not guilty, but he suffered for those who are guilty to bring you to God."

1 PETER 3:18

Christ came to earth for one reason: to give his life as a ransom.... He went to the cross, where man's utter despair collided with God's unbending grace. And in that moment when God's great gift was complete, the compassionate Christ showed the world the cost of his gift.... He who was perfect gave that perfect record to us, and our imperfect record was given to him.... As a result, God's holiness is honored and his children are forgiven.

MARCH 6

JUST LIKE JESUS

From this time on we do not think of anyone as the world does.

2 CORINTHIANS 5:16

*A*sk God to help you have his eternal view of the world.... From his perspective
every person is either: Entering through the small gate or the wide gate....
To have a heart like his is to look into the faces of the saved and rejoice!
They are just one grave away from being just like Jesus. To have a heart like
his is to look into the faces of the lost and pray. For unless they turn,
they are one grave away from torment.

OCTOBER 27

HE STILL MOVES STONES

May the God you serve all the time save you!

DANIEL 6:16

$\mathcal{L}$ook at Jonah in the fish belly.... He prays.... Before he can say amen...the fish belches, and Jonah lands face first on the beach. Look at Daniel in the lions' den; his prospects aren't much better than Jonah's.... Or look at Joseph in the pit.... Though the road to the palace takes a detour through a prison, it eventually ends up at the throne.... Such are the stories in the Bible. One near-death experience after another. Just when the neck is on the chopping block...Calvary comes.

MARCH 7

A GENTLE THUNDER

*My God will use his wonderful riches in Christ Jesus
to give you everything you need.*

PHILIPPIANS 4:19

God's faithfulness has never depended on the faithfulness of his children.
He is faithful even when we aren't.... When the disciples didn't pray, Jesus prayed.
When the disciples didn't see God, Jesus sought God. When the disciples were
weak, Jesus was strong. When the disciples had no faith, Jesus had faith. I simply
think God is greater than our weakness. In fact, I think it is our weakness
that reveals how great God is.... God is faithful even when his children are not.

OCTOBER 26

WHEN GOD WHISPERS YOUR NAME

The true children of God are those who let God's Spirit lead them.

ROMANS 8:14

We talk about the Father and study the Son—but when it comes to the Holy Spirit, we are confused at best and frightened at worst. May I simplify things a bit? The Holy Spirit is the presence of God in our lives, carrying on the work of Jesus. The Holy Spirit helps us in three directions—inwardly (by granting us the fruits of the Spirit), upwardly (by praying for us) and outwardly (by pouring God's love into our hearts).

MARCH 8

WALKING WITH THE SAVIOR

Where God's love is, there is no fear, because God's perfect love drives out fear.

1 JOHN 4:18

Somewhere, sometime, some [thing] convinced us that...God's going to nail us when we've gone too far. No concept could be more wrong! Our Savior's Father is very fond of us and only wants to share his love with us. We have a Father who is filled with compassion, a feeling Father who hurts when his children hurt. We serve a God who says that even when we...feel like nothing is going to go right, he is waiting for us, to embrace us whether we succeed or fail.

OCTOBER 25

THE GREAT HOUSE OF GOD

May your kingdom come and what you want be done,
here on earth as it is in heaven.

MATTHEW 6:10

"Thy will be done" is to seek the heart of God.... He wants you to know it.... Could he have done more than send his Son to lead us? Could he have done more than give his word to teach us?... Could he have done more than send his Holy Spirit to counsel us? Wherever he sees sincere seekers with confused hearts, you can bet...he will do whatever it takes to help them see his will.

MARCH 9

A GENTLE THUNDER

If anyone belongs to Christ, there is a new creation.
The old things have gone; everything is made new!

2 CORINTHIANS 5:17

*H*ave you been there? Have you felt the ground of conviction give way
beneath your feet? The ledge crumbles, your eyes widen, and down you go. Poof!
Now what do you do?... When we fall, we can dismiss it. We can deny it.
We can distort it. Or we can deal with it.... We keep no secrets from God.
Confession is not telling God what we did. He already knows. Confession
is simply agreeing with God that our acts were wrong.

OCTOBER 24

A GENTLE THUNDER

God even knows how many hairs are on your head.

MATTHEW 10:30

*I*f God had a refrigerator, your picture would be on it. If he had a wallet, your photo would be in it. He sends you flowers every spring and a sunrise every morning. Whenever you want to talk, he'll listen. He can live anywhere in the universe, and he chose your heart.... Face it, friend. He's crazy about you.

MARCH 10

JUST LIKE JESUS

There is joy in the presence of the angels of God when one sinner changes his heart and life.

LUKE 15:10

Why do Jesus and his angels rejoice over one repenting sinner? Can they see something we can't? Do they know something we don't? Absolutely. They know what heaven holds…. Heaven is populated by those who let God change them…. Every sin is gone. Every insecurity is forgotten. Every fear is past…. Pure love. No lust. Pure hope. No fear. No wonder the angels rejoice when one sinner repents; they know another work of art will soon grace the gallery of God. They know what heaven holds.

OCTOBER 23

JUST LIKE JESUS

*Be kind and loving to each other, and forgive each other
just as God forgave you in Christ.*

EPHESIANS 4:32

[*Jesus*] takes up the basin, and kneels before one of the disciples.... One by
one...Jesus works his way down the row.... Jesus knows the future of these feet he
is washing. These twenty-four feet will not spend the next day following their
master.... He knows what these men are about to do.... And when they do,
he wants them to remember how...he washed their feet. He wants them to realize
those feet are still clean.... He forgave their sin before they even committed it.

MARCH 11

JUST LIKE JESUS

*He who overcomes, and keeps My works until the end,
to him I will give power over the nations.*

REVELATION 2:26

What if God weren't here on earth? You think people can be cruel now,
imagine us without the presence of God. You think we are brutal to each other
now, imagine the world without the Holy Spirit. You think there is loneliness
and despair and guilt now, imagine life without the touch of Jesus.... If God took
away his angels, his grace, his promise of eternity, and his servants, what would
the world be like? In a word, hell.

OCTOBER 22

IN THE GRIP OF GRACE

Now you are free from sin and have become slaves of God. This brings you a life that is only for God, and this gives you life forever.

ROMANS 6:22

*H*ow could we who have been freed from sin return to it? Before Christ our lives were out of control, sloppy, and indulgent. We didn't even know we were slobs until we met him. Then he moved in. Things began to change.... Suddenly we find ourselves wanting to do good. Go back to the old mess? Are you kidding?

MARCH 12

IN THE EYE OF THE STORM

Lord, even when I have trouble all around me,
you will keep me alive.

PSALM 138:7

There is a window in your heart through which you can see God. Once upon a time that window was clear.... You could see God as vividly as you could see a gentle valley or hillside. Then, suddenly, the window cracked. A pebble broke the window. A pebble of pain. And suddenly God was not so easy to see.... You were puzzled. God wouldn't allow something like this to happen, would he? When you can't see him, trust him.... Jesus is closer than you've ever dreamed.

OCTOBER 21

HE STILL MOVES STONES

Seek God's kingdom, and all the other things you need
will be given to you.

LUKE 12:31

Sometimes God is so touched by what he sees that he gives us what we need
and not simply that for which we ask. It's a good thing. For who would have ever
thought to ask God for what he gives?... Jesus already knows the cost of grace.
He already knows the price of forgiveness. But he offers it anyway.
Love burst his heart.

MARCH 13

HE STILL MOVES STONES

Faith that does nothing is dead!

JAMES 2:26

Faith is not the belief that God will do what you want. Faith is the belief that
God will do what is right. God is always near and always available. Just waiting
for your touch. So let him know. Demonstrate your devotion: Write a letter.
Ask forgiveness. Be baptized. Feed a hungry person. Pray. Teach. Go.
Do something that demonstrates faith. For faith with no effort is no faith at all.
God will respond. He has never rejected a genuine gesture of faith. Never.

OCTOBER 20

WHEN CHRIST COMES

*The One who died for us...is in the presence of God
at this very moment sticking up for us.*

ROMANS 8:34 THE MESSAGE

Jesus is praying for us.... Jesus has spoken and Satan has listened. The devil may land a punch or two. He may even win a few rounds, but he never wins the fight. Why? Because Jesus takes up for you.... Jesus, at this very moment, is protecting you.... And God will "never let you be pushed past your limit; he'll always be there to help you come through it" (1 Corinthians 10:13 THE MESSAGE).

MARCH 14

IN THE EYE OF THE STORM

*To choose life is to love the Lord your God, obey him,
and stay close to him.*

DEUTERONOMY 30:20

*H*e placed one scoop of clay upon another until a form lay lifeless on the
ground.... All were silent as the Creator reached in himself and removed
something yet unseen. "It's called 'choice.' The seed of choice." Within the man,
God had placed a divine seed. A seed of his self. The God of might had created
earth's mightiest. The Creator had created, not a creature, but another creator.
And the One who had chosen to love had created one who could love in return.
Now it's our choice.

OCTOBER 19

THE GREAT HOUSE OF GOD

*When [the disciples] saw who he was, he disappeared. They said
to each other, "It felt like a fire burning in us when Jesus talked
to us on the road and explained the Scriptures to us."*

LUKE 24:31-32

*D*on't you love that verse? They knew they had been with Jesus because
of the fire within them. God reveals his will by setting a torch to your soul....
Jesus comes to set you on fire! He walks as a torch from heart to heart,
warming the cold and thawing the chilled and stirring the ashes.

MARCH 15

WHEN CHRIST COMES

*The Lord comforts his people and will have pity
on those who suffer.*

ISAIAH 49:13

[God] speaks to all of us who have stood or will stand in the soft dirt near
an open grave.... "I want you to know what happens to a Christian when he dies
so that when it happens, you will not be full of sorrow, as those are who have
no hope. For since we believe that Jesus died and then came back to life again,
we can also believe that when Jesus returns, God will bring back with him
all the Christians who have died" (1 Thessalonians 4:13–14 TLB).

OCTOBER 18

IN THE EYE OF THE STORM

Never will I leave you; never will I forsake you.

HEBREWS 13:5 NIV

There is never a time during which Jesus is not speaking. Never. There is never a place in which Jesus is not present. Never. There is never a room so dark...that the ever-present, ever-pursuing, relentlessly tender Friend is not there, tapping gently on the doors of our hearts—waiting to be invited in.... But never interpret our numbness as his absence.... There is no chorus so loud that the voice of God cannot be heard...if we will but listen.

MARCH 16

IN THE EYE OF THE STORM

*We do not make requests of you because we are righteous,
but because of your great mercy.*

DANIEL 9:18 NIV

We prefer to get salvation the old-fashioned way: We earn it. To accept grace is to admit failure, a step we are hesitant to take. We opt to impress God with how good we are rather than confessing how great he is.... Think that God will smile on our efforts. He doesn't. God's smile is not for the healthy hiker who boasts that he made the journey alone. It is, instead, for the crippled leper who begs God for a back on which to ride.

OCTOBER 17

THE APPLAUSE OF HEAVEN

I want to know Christ and the power that raised him from the dead.

PHILIPPIANS 3:10

*T*race the path of this Savior, the God who swapped heavenly royalty for earthly poverty.... He was dependent on handouts for his income.... He knew what it meant to have no home.... His friends weren't always faithful to him. He was accused of a crime he never committed.... A judge swayed by politics handed down the death penalty. They killed him. And why? Because of the gift that only he could give.

MARCH 17

JUST LIKE JESUS

Rejoice that your names are written in heaven.

LUKE 10:20 NIV

$\mathcal{L}$et a child call and the ear of the Father inclines.... And, most important, let a sinner repent, and every other activity ceases, and every heavenly being celebrates.... When you hear of a soul saved, do you drop everything and celebrate? Is your good day made better or your bad day salvaged? We may be pleased—but exuberant?... When a soul is saved, the heart of Jesus becomes the night sky on the Fourth of July, radiant with explosions of cheer. Can the same be said about us?

OCTOBER 16

WALKING WITH THE SAVIOR

Everyone who is a child of God conquers the world.
And this is the victory that conquers the world—our faith.

1 JOHN 5:4

You get impatient with your own life, trying to master a habit or control a sin—
and in your frustration begin to wonder where the power of God is. Be patient.
God is using today's difficulties to strengthen you for tomorrow. He is equipping
you. The God who makes things grow will help you bear fruit.... After all,
regardless of what you do, God does what is right: he saves you with his grace.

MARCH 18

THE INSPIRATIONAL STUDY BIBLE

*In the beginning there was the Word. The Word was with God,
and the Word was God.*

JOHN 1:1

𝒩ot only has [the Bible] survived, it has thrived. It is the single most popular book in all of history.... The Bible's durability is not found on earth; it is found in heaven. For the millions who have tested its claims and claimed its promises there is but one answer—the Bible is God's book and God's voice.... The purpose of the Bible is to proclaim God's plan and passion to save his children.... It is the treasure map that leads us to God's highest treasure, eternal life.

OCTOBER 15

JUST LIKE JESUS

The blood of Jesus, God's Son, cleanses us from every sin.

1 JOHN 1:7

We are always being cleansed. The cleansing is not a promise for the future but a reality in the present.... Our Savior kneels down and gazes upon the darkest acts of our lives. But rather than recoil in horror, he reaches out in kindness and says, "I can clean that if you want."... But that's not all he does. Because he lives in us, you and I can do the same. Because he has forgiven us, we can forgive others.

MARCH 19

THE GREAT HOUSE OF GOD

*God is spirit, and those who worship him must worship
in spirit and truth.*

JOHN 4:24

Since God is Spirit (John 4:23), he is next to you.... Moses knew this. "Lord,"
he prayed, "you have been our home since the beginning" (Psalm 90:1).
What a powerful thought: God as your home. Your home is the place where
you can kick off your shoes.... Your home is familiar to you.... God can be equally
familiar to you. With time you can learn where to go for nourishment, where
to hide for protection, where to turn for guidance. Just as your earthly house
is a place of refuge, so God's house is a place of peace.

OCTOBER 14

HE STILL MOVES STONES

God made you alive with Christ, and he forgave all your sins.
He canceled the debt, which listed all the rules we failed to follow.

COLOSSIANS 2:13-14

*A*ll the world religions can be placed in one of two camps: legalism or grace....
A legalist believes the...brunt of responsibility doesn't lie within God; it lies
within you. The result? The outside sparkles.... But look closely.... Something is
missing.... Spiritual life is not a human endeavor. It is rooted in and orchestrated
by the Holy Spirit. Every spiritual achievement is created and energized by God.

MARCH 20

A GENTLE THUNDER

*Being made right with God by his grace, we could have the hope
of receiving the life that never ends.*

TITUS 3:7

You may be decent.... But apart from Christ you aren't holy. So how can
you go to heaven? Only believe. Accept the work already done, the work of Jesus
on the cross.... Stand before God in his name, not yours. It's that easy? There was
nothing easy about it at all. The cross was heavy, the blood was real, and the price
was extravagant. It would have bankrupted you or me, so he paid it for us....
Call it what it is. Call it grace.

OCTOBER 13

THE GREAT HOUSE OF GOD

The Lord hears good people when they cry out to him,
and he saves them from all their troubles.

PSALM 34:17

*W*hen [a friend] told Jesus of the illness [of Lazarus] he said, "Lord, the one you love is sick." He doesn't base his appeal on the imperfect love of the one in need, but on the perfect love of the Savior.... The power of the prayer...does not depend on the one who makes the prayer, but on the one who hears the prayer.... The Savior hears the prayer. He silences heaven, so he won't miss a word.

MARCH 21

PREFACE, GRACE FOR THE MOMENT

Let us boldly approach the throne of our gracious God, where we may receive mercy and his grace to find timely help.

HEBREWS 4:16 NEB

*D*id you note those last two words? "Timely help." Not too soon, nor too late. Just on time. Just as it's my job to make sure my children have what they need, God will make sure you have what you need. From his hand you will receive.

OCTOBER 12

IN THE EYE OF THE STORM

*Pray for all people, asking God for what they need
and being thankful to him.*

1 TIMOTHY 2:1

The disciples must have asked [questions] in the storm. All they could see
were black skies as they bounced in the battered boat.... [Then] a figure came
to them walking on the water. It wasn't what they expected.... They almost
missed seeing the answer to their prayers. And unless we look and listen closely,
we risk making the same mistake. God's lights in our dark nights are
as numerous as the stars, if only we'll look for them.

MARCH 22

HE STILL MOVES STONES

He is a faithful God who does no wrong, who is right and fair.

DEUTERONOMY 32:4

To recognize God as Lord is to acknowledge that he is sovereign and supreme in the universe. To accept him as Savior is to accept his gift of salvation offered on the cross. To regard him as Father is to go a step further. Ideally, a father is the one in your life who provides and protects. This is exactly what God has done....

God has proven himself as a faithful father. Now it falls to us
to be trusting children.

OCTOBER 11

NO WONDER THEY CALL HIM THE SAVIOR

*During the days of Jesus' life on earth, he offered up prayers
and petitions with loud cries and tears to the one who could
save him from death.*

HEBREWS 5:7

*M*y, what a portrait!... Jesus is cloaked, not in sainthood, but in humanity....
The next time your self-pity convinces you that no one cares, pay a visit
to Gethsemane. And the next time you wonder if God really perceives
the pain that prevails on this dusty planet, listen to him pleading
among the twisted trees.

MARCH 23

JUST LIKE JESUS

*Wish good for those who harm you; wish them well
and do not curse them.*

ROMANS 12:14

The Bible says, "Judas...was a thief" (John 12:6). The man was a crook.
Somehow he was able to live in the presence of God and...remain unchanged.
In the end he decided he'd rather have money than a friend.... Judas was a
scoundrel, a cheat, and a bum.... What Jesus saw in Judas as worthy of being
called a friend, I can't imagine. But I do know that Jesus doesn't lie,
and in that moment he saw something good in a very bad man....
He can help us do the same with those who hurt us.

OCTOBER 10

HE STILL MOVES STONES

We are made holy through the sacrifice Christ made in his body once and for all time.

HEBREWS 10:10

*O*nly the holy will see God.... Perfection is a requirement for eternity. We wish it weren't so. We act like it isn't so. We act like those who are "decent" will see God. Sounds right to us, but it doesn't sound right to God.... God is the standard for perfection. We don't compare ourselves to others; they are just as fouled up as we are. The goal is to be like him; anything less is inadequate.

MARCH 24

WHEN CHRIST COMES

The day of the Lord will come like a thief. The skies will disappear with a loud noise.... So what kind of people should you be?

2 PETER 3:10-11

Great question.... Peter tells us: "You should live holy lives and serve God, as you wait for and look forward to the coming of the day of God" (vv. 11–12).... Let us wait forwardly, but let us wait.... We are so good at waiting that we don't wait forwardly. We forget to look.... We are too content...We seldom, if ever, allow the Holy Spirit to interrupt our plans and lead us to worship so that we might see Jesus.

OCTOBER 9

WHEN CHRIST COMES

"In [this] world you will have tribulation," Jesus promises,
"but be of good cheer, I have overcome the world."

JOHN 16:33 NKJV

*G*od has kept no secrets. He has told us that...we will experience trouble....
But just because the devil shows up and cackles, we needn't panic.... Our Master
speaks of an accomplished deed.... "It is finished" (John 19:30). The battle is over.
Be alert. But don't be alarmed.... Satan is loosed for a season, but the season is
oh-so-brief.... Just a few more scenes, just a few more turns in the road,
and his end will come.

MARCH 25

THE GREAT HOUSE OF GOD

Those who go to God Most High for safety will be protected by the Almighty.

PSALM 91:1

We create elaborate houses for our bodies, but our souls are relegated to a hillside shanty where the night winds chill us and the rain soaks us.... We don't have to live outside.... God wants you to move in out of the cold and live...with him. Under his roof there is space available. At his table a plate is set. In his living room a wingback chair is reserved just for you. And he'd like you to take up residence in his house. Why...? Simple, he's your Father.

OCTOBER 8

JUST LIKE JESUS

*Jesus reached out his hand and touched the man and said,
"I will. Be healed!"*

MATTHEW 8:3

Oh, the power of a godly touch. Haven't you known it?... Can't we offer
the same? Many of you already do. Some of you have the master touch
of the Physician himself. You use your hands to pray over the sick and minister
to the weak. If you aren't touching them personally, your hands are writing
letters, dialing phones, baking pies. You have learned the power
of a touch.

MARCH 26

"HE REMINDED US OF YOU"

Let us always offer to God our sacrifice of praise.

HEBREWS 13:15

You are a great God. Your character is holy. Your truth is absolute. Your strength is unending. Your discipline is fair.... Your provisions are abundant for our needs. Your light is adequate for our path. Your grace is sufficient for our sins.... You are never early, never late.... You sent your Son in the fullness of time and will return at the consummation of time. Your plan is perfect. Bewildering. Puzzling. Troubling. But perfect.

OCTOBER 7

THE GREAT HOUSE OF GOD

Depend on the Lord; trust him, and he will take care of you.

PSALM 37:5

God is committed to caring for our needs. Paul tells us that a man who won't feed his own family is worse than an unbeliever (1 Timothy 5:8). How much more will a holy God care for his children? After all, how can we fulfill his mission unless our needs are met? How can we teach or minister or influence unless we have our basic needs satisfied? Will God enlist us in his army and not provide a commissary? Of course not.

MARCH 27

HE STILL MOVES STONES

As many as walk according to this rule, peace and mercy be upon them.

GALATIANS 6:16

*A*s we get older, our vision should improve. Not our vision of earth, but our vision of heaven. Those who have spent their life looking for heaven gain a skip in their step as the city comes into view. After Michelangelo died, someone found in his studio a...note to his apprentice.... The great artist wrote: "Draw, Antonio, draw, and do not waste time." Well-founded urgency, Michelangelo. Time slips. Days pass. Years fade. And life ends. And what we came to do must be done while there is time.

OCTOBER 6

HE STILL MOVES STONES

*The Father has loved us so much that we are called children
of God. And we really are his children.*

1 JOHN 3:1

Let me tell you who you are. In fact, let me proclaim who you are. You are an
heir of God and a co-heir with Christ. You are eternal, like an angel. You have
a crown that will last forever. You are a holy priest, a treasured possession....
But more than any of the above...is the simple fact that you are God's child....
As a result, if something is important to you, it's important to God.

MARCH 28

WHEN CHRIST COMES

For to me, to live is Christ and to die is gain.

PHILIPPIANS 1:21 NIV

*J*ust as a parent needs to know that his or her child is safe at school, we long to know that our loved ones are safe in death.... When speaking about the period between the death of the body and the resurrection of the body, the Bible doesn't shout; it just whispers. But at the confluence of these whispers, a firm voice is heard. This authoritative voice assures us that, at death, the Christian immediately enters into the presence of God and enjoys conscious fellowship with the Father and with those who have gone before.

OCTOBER 5

THE INSPIRATIONAL STUDY BIBLE

All people will know that you are my followers
if you love each other.

JOHN 13:35

*W*atch a small boy follow his dad through the snow. He stretches to step where his dad stepped. Not an easy task. His small legs extend as far as they can so his feet can fall in his father's prints. The father, seeing what the son is doing, smiles and begins taking shorter steps, so the son can follow. It's a picture of discipleship.

MARCH 29

IN THE EYE OF THE STORM

[Peter] shouted, "Lord, save me!" Immediately Jesus reached out his hand and caught Peter.

MATTHEW 14:30-31

*W*e come to Christ in an hour of deep need. We abandon the boat of good works.... We realize, like Peter, that spanning the gap between us and Jesus is a feat too great for our feet. So we beg for help. Hear his voice. And step out in fear, hoping that our little faith will be enough.... Faith is a desperate dive out of the sinking boat of human effort and a prayer that God will be there to pull us out of the water.

OCTOBER 4

SIX HOURS ONE FRIDAY

He humbled himself and was fully obedient to God,
even when that caused his death—death on a cross.

PHILIPPIANS 2:8

When human hands fastened the divine hands to a cross with spikes, it wasn't the soldiers who held the hands of Jesus steady. It was God who held them steady.... Take a stroll out to the hill. Out to Calvary. Out to the cross where, with holy blood, the hand that placed you on the planet wrote the promise, "God would give up his only Son before he'd give up on you."

MARCH 30

JUST LIKE JESUS

If people's thinking is controlled by the sinful self, there is death.
But if their thinking is controlled by the Spirit,
there is life and peace.

ROMANS 8:6

*Y*our mind is the doorway to your heart.... The Holy Spirit is ready to help
you manage and filter the thoughts that try to enter. He can help you guard
your heart. He stands with you on the threshold. A thought approaches,
a questionable thought. Do you throw open the door and let it enter?
Of course not. You "fight to capture every thought until it acknowledges
the authority of Christ" (2 Corinthians 10:5 PHILLIPS).

OCTOBER 3

IN THE EYE OF THE STORM

A time is coming when all...will hear his voice and come out—
those who have done good will rise to live.

JOHN 5:28-29 NIV

A day is coming when everyone will hear [Jesus'] voice. Some will hear his voice for the very first time. It's not that he never spoke, it's just that they never listened.... But others will be called...by a familiar voice.... They are servants who opened the door when Jesus knocked. Now the door will open again. Only this time, it won't be Jesus who walks into our house; it will be we, who walk into his.

MARCH 31

IN THE GRIP OF GRACE

It is not our love for God; it is God's love for us in sending his Son to be the way to take away our sins.

1 JOHN 4:10

We have attempted to scale the Everest of salvation, but we have yet to leave the base camp, much less ascend the slope. The quest is simply too great; we don't need more supplies or muscle or technique; we need a helicopter. Can't you hear it hovering? "God has a way to make people right with him" (Romans 3:21). How vital that we embrace this truth.... God's dream is to make us right with him.

OCTOBER 2

GOD CAME NEAR

[They] put him to death by nailing him to a cross.
But this was God's plan which he had made long ago.

ACTS 2:23

*T*he cross was no accident.... The death of the Son of God was anything
but an unexpected peril. No it was part of an incredible plan. A calculated
choice. The moment the forbidden fruit touched the lips of Eve, the shadow
of a cross appeared on the horizon. And between that moment and the moment
the man with the mallet placed the spike against the wrist of God,
a master plan was fulfilled.

APRIL 1

IN THE GRIP OF GRACE

We are many, but in Christ we are all one body.
Each one is a part of that body.

ROMANS 12:5

$\mathcal{G}$od has enlisted us in his navy and placed us on his ship...to carry us safely
to the other shore. This is...a battleship.... Each of us has a different task.
Some...are snatching people from the water. Others...man the cannons of prayer
and worship. Still others devote themselves to the crew.... Each can tell of a
personal encounter with the captain, for each has received a personal call....
We each followed him across the gangplank of his grace onto the same boat.

OCTOBER 1

GOD CAME NEAR

Jesus was born crucified. Whenever he became conscious of who he was, he also became conscious of what he had to do. The cross-shaped shadow could always be seen.... This explains the resoluteness in the words, "The reason my Father loves me is that I lay down my life—only to take it up again. No one takes it from me, but I lay it down of my own accord" (John 10:17–18 NIV).... So call it what you wish: An act of grace. A plan of redemption.... But whatever you call it, don't call it an accident. It was anything but that.

APRIL 2

THE GREAT HOUSE OF GOD

*Remember, O Lord, Your tender mercies and Your
lovingkindnesses, for they are from of old.*

PSALM 25:6

One afternoon,...we found ourselves behind an orthodox Jewish family—
a father and his three small girls. One of the daughters...fell a few steps behind
and couldn't see her father. "Abba!" she called to him. He spotted her and
immediately extended his hand.... Isn't that what we all need? An abba who
will hear when we call? Who will take our hand when we are weak?...
Don't we all need an abba who will swing us up into his arms
and carry us home? We all need a father.

SEPTEMBER 30

AND THE ANGELS WERE SILENT

Then Jesus went about a stone's throw away from them.
He kneeled down and prayed.

LUKE 22:41

*T*he final prayer of Jesus was about you. His final pain was for you.
His final passion was for you. Before he went to the cross, Jesus went to the
garden. And when he spoke with his Father, you were in his prayers....
And God couldn't turn his back on you....
On the eve of the cross, Jesus made his decision. He would rather
go to hell for you than go to heaven without you.

APRIL 3

WALKING WITH THE SAVIOR

Death, where is your victory? Death, where is your pain?

1 CORINTHIANS 15:55

The fire that lit the boiler of the New Testament church was an unquenchable belief that if Jesus had been only a man, he would have stayed in the tomb.... Let us ask our Father humbly, yet confidently in the name of Jesus, to remind us of the empty tomb. Let us see the victorious Jesus: the conqueror of the tomb, the one who defied death. And let us be reminded that we, too, will be granted that same victory!

SEPTEMBER 29

WALKING WITH THE SAVIOR

Though your sins are like scarlet, they can be as white as snow.
Though your sins are deep red, they can be white like wool.

ISAIAH 1:18

When Jesus told us to pray for forgiveness of our debts as we forgive our own debtors, he knew who would be the one to pay the debt.... You are forgiven. If you are in Christ, when he sees you, your sins are covered—he doesn't see them. He sees you better than you see yourself. And that is a glorious fact of your life.

APRIL 4

JUST LIKE JESUS

Be careful what you think, because your thoughts run your life.

PROVERBS 4:23

[God] wants you to "think and act like Christ Jesus" (Philippians 2:5). But how? The answer is surprisingly simple. We can be transformed if we make one decision: I will submit my thoughts to the authority of Jesus.... Jesus claims to be the CEO of heaven and earth. He has the ultimate say on everything, especially our thoughts.... To have a pure heart, we must submit all thoughts to the authority of Christ. If we are willing to do that, he will change us to be like him.

SEPTEMBER 28

THE INSPIRATIONAL STUDY BIBLE

Come, let's worship him and bow down.
Let's kneel before the Lord who made us.

PSALM 95:6

*W*orship. In two thousand years we haven't worked out the kinks.
We still struggle for the right words in prayer. We still fumble over Scripture....
Worship is a daunting task. For that reason, God gave us the Psalms—a praise
book for God's people.... This collection of hymns and petitions are strung
together by one thread—a heart hungry for God.... Worship is personal.
No secret formula exists. What moves you may stymie another.
Each worships differently. But each should worship.

APRIL 5

THE INSPIRATIONAL STUDY BIBLE

*Surely I spoke of things I did not understand; I talked of things
too wonderful for me to know.*

JOB 42:3

*I*t's easy to thank God when he does what we want. But God doesn't always do
what we want. Ask Job. His empire collapsed, his children were killed, and what
was a healthy body became a rage of boils.... Job goes straight to God and pleads
his case.... And God answers.... The point is this: God owes no one anything.
No reasons. No explanations. Nothing.... God is God. He knows what he
is doing. When you can't trace his hand, trust his heart.

SEPTEMBER 27

IN THE EYE OF THE STORM

*I pray these things while I am still in the world so that these
followers can have all of my joy in them.*

JOHN 17:13

*J*esus prayed. We don't know what he prayed about. But I have my guesses....
He prayed for the impossible to happen. Or maybe I'm wrong. Maybe he didn't
ask for anything. Maybe he just stood quietly in the presence of Presence
and basked in the Majesty. Perhaps he placed his war-weary self before the
throne and rested. Maybe he lifted his head out of the confusion of earth
long enough to hear the solution of heaven.

APRIL 6

THE APPLAUSE OF HEAVEN

Rejoice and be glad, because you have a great reward waiting for you in heaven.

MATTHEW 5:12

*M*atthew 5 describes God's radical reconstruction of the heart.... First, we recognize we are in need (we're poor in spirit). Next, we repent of our self-sufficiency (we mourn). We...surrender control to God (we're meek). So grateful are we for his presence that we yearn for more of him (we hunger and thirst).... We forgive others (we're merciful). We change our outlook (we're pure in heart). We love others (we're peace-makers). We endure injustice (we're persecuted). It's no casual shift of attitude.... The more radical the change, the greater the joy.

SEPTEMBER 26

A GENTLE THUNDER

I have given you power...that is greater than the enemy has.

LUKE 10:19

*M*any players appear on the stage of Gethsemane.... [But] the encounter is...between God and Satan. Satan dares to enter yet another garden, but God stands and Satan hasn't a prayer.... Satan falls in the presence of Christ.... Satan is silent in the proclamation of Christ.... Satan is powerless against the protection of Christ.... When Jesus says he will keep you safe, he means it.... When he says he will get you home, he will get you home.

APRIL 7

WHEN GOD WHISPERS YOUR NAME

I will also give to each one who wins the victory a white stone with a new name written on it.

REVELATION 2:17

Makes sense. Fathers are fond of giving their children special names. Princess. Tiger. Sweetheart.... Isn't it incredible to think that God has saved a name just for you? One you don't even know?... Your eternity is so special no common name will do. So God has one reserved just for you. There is more to your life than you ever thought. There is more to your story than what you have read.... And so I plead.... Be there when God whispers your name.

SEPTEMBER 25

WHEN GOD WHISPERS YOUR NAME

Be strong in the Lord and in his great power.

EPHESIANS 6:10

$\mathcal{I}$ stand a few feet from a mirror and see the face of a man who failed,... who failed his Maker. Again. I promised I wouldn't, but I did.... If this were the first time, it would be different. But it isn't.... Your eyes look in the mirror and see a sinner, a failure, a promise-breaker. But by faith you look in the mirror and see a robed prodigal bearing the ring of grace on your finger and the kiss of your Father on your face.

APRIL 8

WHEN CHRIST COMES

Everyone who lives and believes in me will never die.

JOHN 11:26

Whether it be at a school or a cemetery, separation is tough. It is right for us to weep, but there is no need for us to despair.... You and I might wonder why God took them home. But they don't. They understand. They are, at this very moment, at peace in the presence of God.... When it is cold on earth, we can take comfort in knowing that our loved ones are in the warm arms of God. And when Christ comes, we will hold them, too.

SEPTEMBER 24

THE APPLAUSE OF HEAVEN

*Christ's love is greater than anyone can ever know,
but I pray that you will be able to know that love.*

EPHESIANS 3:19

It wasn't right that spikes pierced the hands that formed the earth. And it wasn't right that the Son of God was forced to hear the silence of God.... He sat in silence while the sins of the world were placed upon his Son. And he did nothing while a cry...echoed in the black sky: "My God, my God, why have you forsaken me?" Was it right? No. Was it fair? No. Was it love? Yes.

APRIL 9

WHEN CHRIST COMES

Don't let your hearts be troubled. Trust in God, and trust in me.

JOHN 14:1

*O*ur [little] minds are ill-equipped to handle the thoughts of eternity....
Consequently, our Lord takes the posture of a parent.... Trust me.... Don't be
troubled by the return of Christ. Don't be anxious about things you cannot
comprehend.... For the Christian, the return of Christ is not a riddle to be
solved or a code to be broken, but rather a day to be anticipated.

SEPTEMBER 23

NO WONDER THEY CALL HIM THE SAVIOR

When he saw the crowds, he felt sorry for them because they were hurting and helpless, like sheep without a shepherd.

MATTHEW 9:36

Why did Jesus [die on the cross]? Oh, I know, I know. I have heard the official answers. "To gratify the old law." "To fulfill prophecy."... But there is something more here.... Something personal. What is it?... Could it be that his heart was broken for the hurting?... I imagine him, bending close to those who hurt. I imagine him listening.... He who also was once alone, understands.

APRIL 10

IN THE EYE OF THE STORM

Lord, show us the Father. That is all we need.

JOHN 14:8

*B*iographies of bold disciples begin with chapters of honest terror. Fear of death. Fear of failure. Fear of loneliness. Fear of a wasted life. Fear of failing to know God. Faith begins when you see God on the mountain and you are in the valley and you know that you're too weak to make the climb.... Paul had mastered the Law. He had mastered the system. But one glimpse of God convinced him that sacrifice and symbols were not enough.... Faith that begins with fear will end up nearer the Father.

SEPTEMBER 22

NO WONDER THEY CALL HIM THE SAVIOR

When Jesus tasted the vinegar, he said, "It is finished."
Then he bowed his head and died.

JOHN 19:30

"It is finished." Stop and listen a moment. Let the words wind through your heart.... Jesus draws in a deep breath, pushes his feet down on that Roman nail, and cries, "It is finished!" What was finished? The history-long plan of redeeming man was finished. The message of God to man was finished. The works done by Jesus as a man on earth were finished.... The sting of death had been removed. It was over.

APRIL 11

JUST LIKE JESUS

The devil, your enemy, goes around like a roaring lion looking for someone to eat. Refuse to give in to him, by standing strong in your faith.

1 PETER 5:8-9

For most of us, thought management is, well, unthought of. We think much about time management, weight management, personnel management.... But what about thought management? Shouldn't we be as concerned about managing our thoughts as we are managing anything else? Jesus was. Like a trained soldier at the gate of a city, he stood watch over his mind. He stubbornly guarded the gateway of his heart.... If he did, shouldn't we?

SEPTEMBER 21

IN THE EYE OF THE STORM

God loved the world so much that he gave his one and only Son so that whoever believes in him may not be lost, but have eternal life.

JOHN 3:16

*H*e looked around the hill and foresaw a scene. Three figures hung on three crosses. Arms spread. Heads fallen forward. They moaned with the wind.... All heaven stood to fight.... All eternity poised to protect. But the Creator gave no command. "It must be done..." he said, and withdrew. The angel spoke again. "It would be less painful...." The Creator interrupted softly. "But it wouldn't be love."

APRIL 12

THE GREAT HOUSE OF GOD

You have not seen Christ, but still you love him.
You cannot see him now, but you believe in him.

1 PETER 1:8

*A*s long as our eyes are on God's majesty there is a bounce in our step.
But let our eyes focus on the dirt beneath us and we will grumble about every
rock and crevice we have to cross. For this reason Paul urged, "Don't shuffle
along, eyes to the ground, absorbed with the things right in front of you.
Look up, and be alert to the things going on around Christ—that's where the
action is. See things from his perspective" (Colossians 3:1–2 THE MESSAGE).

SEPTEMBER 20

WHEN CHRIST COMES

Since Jesus died and broke loose from the grave, God will most certainly bring back to life those who die in Jesus.

1 THESSALONIANS 4:14 THE MESSAGE

The resurrection of Jesus is proof and preview of our own. But...are the claims of the empty tomb true? This is not only a good question. It is *the* question....
In other words, if Christ has been raised, then his followers will join him; but if not, then his followers are fools. The resurrection, then, is the keystone in the arch of the Christian faith.

APRIL 13

WHEN GOD WHISPERS YOUR NAME

May the Lord bless you from Mount Zion, he who made heaven and earth.

PSALM 134:3

*T*he Hebrew writer gives us a National Geographic piece on heaven....
He says when we reach the mountain we will have come to "the city of the
living God.... To the meeting of God's firstborn children whose names are
written in heaven" (Hebrews 12:22–23).... Imagine the meeting of the firstborn.
A gathering of all God's children.... We will be perfect...sinless... And imagine
seeing God. Finally, to gaze in the face of your Father. To feel the Father's gaze
upon you. Neither will ever cease.

SEPTEMBER 19

HE STILL MOVES STONES

At dawn on the first day, Mary Magdalene and another woman named Mary went to look at the tomb.

MATTHEW 28:1

It isn't hope that leads [Mary and Mary Magdalene] up the mountain to the tomb. It is duty. Naked devotion. They expect nothing in return. What could Jesus give? What could a dead man offer? The two women are not climbing the mountain to receive, they are going to the tomb to give. Period. There is no motivation more noble.... Service prompted by duty. This is the call of discipleship.

APRIL 14

IN THE GRIP OF GRACE

Do not be bitter or angry or mad. Never shout angrily or say things to hurt others.

EPHESIANS 4:31

ℒet me be very clear. Hatred will sour your outlook and break your back. The load of bitterness is simply too heavy. Your knees will buckle under the strain, and your heart will break beneath the weight. The mountain before you is steep enough without the heaviness of hatred on your back. The wisest choice—the only choice—is for you to drop the anger. You will never be called upon to give anyone more grace than God has already given you.

SEPTEMBER 18

HE STILL MOVES STONES

Everything you do or say should be done to obey Jesus your Lord.
COLOSSIANS 3:17

Mary and Mary [Magdalene] knew a task had to be done—Jesus' body had to be prepared for burial.... I wonder if halfway to the tomb they had sat down and reconsidered.... What if they had given up?... Whether or not they were tempted to, I'm glad they didn't quit.... You see, we know something they didn't. We know the Father was watching. Mary and Mary thought they were alone. They weren't. They thought their journey was unnoticed. They were wrong. God knew.

APRIL 15

THE GREAT HOUSE OF GOD

The name of the Lord is a strong tower; the righteous run to it and are safe.

PROVERBS 18:10 NKJV

When you are confused about the future, go to your Jehovah-raah, your caring shepherd. When you are anxious about provision, talk to Jehovah-jireh, the Lord who provides. Are your challenges too great? Seek the help of Jehovah-shalom, the Lord is peace. Is your body sick?... Jehovah-rophe, the Lord who heals you, will see you now. Do you feel like a soldier stranded behind enemy lines? Take refuge in Jehovah-nissi, the Lord my banner. Meditating on the names of God reminds you of the character of God.

SEPTEMBER 17

A GENTLE THUNDER

*I am the way, and the truth, and the life. The only way
to the Father is through me.*

JOHN 14:6

Tolerance. A prized virtue today. The ability to be understanding of those
with whom you differ is a sign of sophistication. Jesus, too, was a champion
of tolerance.... But there is one area where Jesus was intolerant.... As far as he was
concerned, when it comes to salvation, there...aren't several paths...there is only
one path. And that path is Jesus himself.

APRIL 16

IN THE GRIP OF GRACE

Lord God All-Powerful, who is like you? Lord, you are powerful and completely trustworthy.

PSALM 89:8

Ponder the achievement of God. He doesn't condone our sin, nor does he compromise his standard. He doesn't ignore our rebellion, nor does he relax his demands. Rather than dismiss our sin, he assumes our sin and, incredibly, sentences himself. God's holiness is honored. Our sin is punished...and we are redeemed. God does what we cannot do so we can be what we dare not dream: perfect before God.

SEPTEMBER 16

THE GREAT HOUSE OF GOD

People cannot do any work that will make them right with God.

ROMANS 4:5

*I*f Christ had not covered us with his grace, each of us would be overdrawn on [our heavenly bank] account.... Our holiness account shows insufficient funds, and only the holy will see the Lord; what can we do? We could try making a few deposits. Maybe if I wave at my neighbor or...go to church next Sunday.... But how do you know when you've made enough?... You are trying to justify an account you can't justify.... "It is God who justifies" (Romans 8:33).

APRIL 17

JUST LIKE JESUS

Speak the truth to one another.

EPHESIANS 4:25 TJB

*A*re you in a dilemma, wondering if you should tell the truth or not?
The question to ask in such moments is, will God bless my deceit?... I don't
think so either. Examine your heart. Ask yourself some tough questions. Am I
being completely honest with my spouse and children?... Am I honest in my
dealings? Am I a trustworthy student? An honest taxpayer?... Do you tell the
truth...always? If not, start today. Don't wait until tomorrow. The ripple
of today's lie is tomorrow's wave and next year's flood.

SEPTEMBER 15

WALKING WITH THE SAVIOR

Christ had no sin, but God made him become sin so that in Christ we could become right with God.

2 CORINTHIANS 5:21

When the one who knew no sin became sin for us...God didn't call his army of angels to save him. He didn't, because he knew he would rather give up his Son than give up on us. Regardless of what you've done...it's not too late.... It's not too late to dig down, pull out that mistake, and then let it go— and be free. What makes a Christian a Christian is not perfection but forgiveness.

APRIL 18

JUST LIKE JESUS

But those who do right will continue to do right, and those whose hands are not dirty with sin will grow stronger.

JOB 17:9

*W*hat if someone were to film a documentary on your hands?... What would we see?... Oh, the power of our hands. Leave them unmanaged and they become weapons: clawing for power, strangling for survival, seducing for pleasure. But manage them and our hands become instruments of grace—not just tools in the hands of God, but God's very hands.

SEPTEMBER 14

HE STILL MOVES STONES

"She will have a son, and they will name him Immanuel,"
which means "God is with us."

MATTHEW 1:23

*T*he white space between Bible verses is fertile soil for questions.
One can hardly read Scripture without whispering, "I wonder...." But in our
wonderings, there is one question we never need to ask. Does God care?
Through the small face of the stable-born baby, he says yes. Yes, your sins
are forgiven. Yes, your name is written in heaven.... And yes, God has
entered your world. Immanuel. God is with us.

APRIL 19

THE APPLAUSE OF HEAVEN

In six days the Lord made everything....
On the seventh day he rested.

EXODUS 20:11

*W*hen I was ten years old, my mother enrolled me in piano lessons....
Spending thirty minutes every afternoon tethered to a piano bench was a
torture.... Some of the music, though, I learned to enjoy.... But there was one
instruction in the music I could never obey to my teacher's satisfaction.
The rest. The zigzagged command to do nothing. What sense does that make?
Why sit at the piano and pause when you can pound?
"Because," my teacher patiently explained, "music is always sweeter after a rest."

SEPTEMBER 13

THE GREAT HOUSE OF GOD

My God, I want to do what you want. Your teachings are in my heart.

PSALM 40:8

*W*ant to know God's will for your life? Then answer this question: What ignites your heart? Forgotten orphans? Untouched nations? The inner city?... Heed the fire within! As a young man I felt the call to preach.... I sought the counsel of a minister I admired.... "Don't preach," he said, "unless you have to." As I pondered his words I found my answer: "I have to. If I don't, the fire will consume me." What is the fire that consumes you?

APRIL 20

WHEN CHRIST COMES

Unless a grain of wheat falls into the earth and dies, it remains a single grain of wheat; but if it dies, it brings a good harvest.

JOHN 12:24 PHILLIPS

We do all we can to live and not die. God, however, says we must die in order to live. When you sow a seed, it must die in the ground before it can grow. What we see as the ultimate tragedy, he sees as the ultimate triumph. And when a Christian dies, it's not a time to despair, but a time to trust.... The seed buried in the earth will blossom in heaven.

SEPTEMBER 12

JUST LIKE JESUS

Jesus often withdrew to lonely places and prayed.

LUKE 5:16 NIV

How long has it been since you let God have you?... How long since you gave him a portion of undiluted, uninterrupted time listening for his voice? Apparently, Jesus did. He made a deliberate effort to spend time with God.... Let me ask the obvious. If Jesus, the Son of God, the sinless Savior of humankind, thought it worthwhile to clear his calendar to pray, wouldn't we be wise to do the same?

APRIL 21

WHEN GOD WHISPERS YOUR NAME

I will ask the Father, and he will give you another Helper to be with you forever—the Spirit of truth.

JOHN 14:16-17

*D*o-it-yourself Christianity is not much encouragement to the done-in and worn-out.... At some point we need more than good advice; we need help. Somewhere on this journey home we realize that a fifty-fifty proposition is too little.... We need help. Help from the inside out.... In the part of us we don't even know. In the heart no one else has seen. In the hidden recesses of our being dwells, not an angel, not a philosophy, not a genie, but God.

SEPTEMBER 11

JUST LIKE JESUS

*We know that when Christ comes, we will be like him,
because we will see him as he really is.*

1 JOHN 3:2

When you arrive [in heaven]...something wonderful will happen.
A final transformation will occur. You will be just like Jesus.... Of all the
blessings of heaven, one of the greatest will be you! You will be God's magnum
opus, his work of art. The angels will gasp. God's work will be completed.
At last, you will have a heart like his.... Your heart will be pure, your words
will be like jewels, your thoughts will be like treasures.

APRIL 22

WHEN GOD WHISPERS YOUR NAME

God has planted eternity in the hearts of men.

ECCLESIASTES 3:10 TLB

It doesn't take a wise person to know that people long for more than earth....
We have our moments. The newborn on our breast, the bride on our arm,
the sunshine on our back.... God flirts with us.... Those moments are appetizers
for the dish that is to come. "No one has ever imagined what God has prepared
for those who love him" (1 Corinthians 2:9). What a breathtaking verse!
Do you see what it says? Heaven is beyond our imagination.... At our most
creative moment, at our deepest thought, at our highest level, we still
cannot fathom eternity.

SEPTEMBER 10

IN THE GRIP OF GRACE

I no longer call you servants,...but I call you friends.

JOHN 15:15

Through Christ's sacrifice, our past is pardoned and our future secure. And, "Since we have been made right with God by our faith, we have peace with God" (Romans 5:1). Peace with God. What a happy consequence of faith! Not just peace between countries, peace between neighbors, or peace at home; salvation brings peace with God.... God is no longer a foe, but a friend. We are at peace with him.

APRIL 23

IN THE EYE OF THE STORM

*About midnight Paul and Silas were praying and singing songs
to God as the other prisoners listened.*

ACTS 16:25

*G*reat acts of faith are seldom born out of calm calculation. It wasn't logic
that caused Moses to raise his staff on the bank of the Red Sea.... And it wasn't
a confident committee that prayed in a small room in Jerusalem for Peter's release
from prison. It was a fearful, desperate, band of backed-into-a-corner believers.
It was a church with no options.... And never were they stronger. At the
beginning of every act of faith, there is often a seed of fear.

SEPTEMBER 9

THE GREAT HOUSE OF GOD

Happy is the person whose sins are forgiven,
whose wrongs are pardoned.

PSALM 32:1

If we are already forgiven, then why does Jesus teach us to pray, "Forgive us our debts"? The very reason you would want your children to do the same. If my children violate one of my standards or disobey a rule, I don't disown them.... But I do expect them to be honest and apologize. And until they do, the tenderness of our relationship will suffer.... The same happens in our walk with God. Confession does not create a relationship with God, it simply nourishes it.

APRIL 24

IN THE EYE OF THE STORM

Each of you has received a gift to use to serve others.

1 PETER 4:10

"Blessed are the meek," Jesus said. The word meek does not mean weak.
It means focused. It is a word used to describe a domesticated stallion. Power
under control.... Blessed are those who recognize their God-given responsibilities.
Blessed are those who acknowledge that there is only one God and have quit
applying for his position. Blessed are those who know what on earth they are
on earth to do and set themselves about the business of doing it.

SEPTEMBER 8

WHEN CHRIST COMES

There are things about him that people cannot see.... But since the beginning of the world those things have been made easy to understand by what God has made.

ROMANS 1:20

God's judgment...is based upon humanity's response to the message received. He will never hold us accountable for what he doesn't tell us. At the same time, he will never let us die without telling us something. Even those who never heard of Christ are given a message about the character of God.... Nature is God's first missionary.... If a person has nothing but nature, then nature is enough to reveal something about God.

APRIL 25

JUST LIKE JESUS

*The Lord hates those who tell lies but is pleased with those
who keep their promises.*

PROVERBS 12:22

*O*ur Master has a strict honor code.... God loves the truth and hates deceit.
In 1 Corinthians 6:9–10 Paul lists the type of people who will not inherit the
kingdom of God...those who sin sexually, worship idols, take part in adultery,
sell their bodies, get drunk, rob people, and—there it is—lie about others....
You mean my fibbing and flattering stir the same heavenly anger as adultery
and aggravated assault? Apparently so.... For one reason: dishonesty is
absolutely contrary to the character of God.

SEPTEMBER 7

THE APPLAUSE OF HEAVEN

All you who put your hope in the Lord be strong and brave.
PSALM 31:24

*H*ow many people do you know who have built a formidable exterior, only to tremble inside with fear?... We face our fears with force...or...we stockpile wealth. We seek security in things. We cultivate fame and seek status. But do these approaches work? Courage is an outgrowth of who we are. Exterior supports may temporarily sustain, but only inward character creates courage.

APRIL 26

JUST LIKE JESUS

No one who is dishonest will live in my house;
no liars will stay around me.

PSALM 101:7

*M*ore than once I've heard people refer to the story [of Ananias and Sapphira]
with a nervous chuckle and say, "I'm glad God doesn't still strike people dead
for lying." I'm not so sure he doesn't. It seems to me that the wages of deceit
is still death. Not death of the body, perhaps, but the death of: a marriage...
a conscience...a career...intimacy, trust, peace, credibility, and self-respect.
But perhaps the most tragic...our [Christian] witness. The court won't listen
to the testimony of a perjured witness. Neither will the world.

SEPTEMBER 6

THE APPLAUSE OF HEAVEN

*You created my inmost being; you knit me together
in my mother's womb.*

PSALM 139:13 NIV

*T*hink on those words. You were knitted together. You aren't an accident.
You weren't mass-produced. You aren't an assembly line product. You were
deliberately planned, specifically gifted, and lovingly positioned on this earth
by the Master Crafts-man.... In a system that ranks the value of a human by the
figures of his salary or the shape of her legs...let me tell you something:
Jesus' plan is a reason for joy!

APRIL 27

HE STILL MOVES STONES

*Let us hold firmly to the hope that we have confessed,
because we can trust God to do what he promised.*

HEBREWS 10:23

*Y*our disappointments too heavy? Read the story of the Emmaus-bound
disciples. The Savior they thought was dead now walked beside them.
He entered their house and sat at their table. And something happened in their
hearts. "It felt like a fire burning in us when Jesus talked to us on the road
and explained the Scriptures to us" (Luke 24:32). Next time you're disappointed,
don't panic. Don't give up. Just be patient and let God remind you he's still
in control.

SEPTEMBER 5

HE STILL MOVES STONES

I tell you the truth, today you will be with me in paradise.

LUKE 23:43

*W*hat has [the thief on the cross] done to warrant help?... Who is he to beg for forgiveness?... What right does he have to pray..., "Jesus remember me when you come into your kingdom"? Do you really want to know? The same right you have to pray.... You see, that is you and me on the cross. Naked, desolate, hopeless, and estranged.... We, like the thief, have one more prayer. And we, like the thief pray. And we, like the thief, hear the voice of grace.

APRIL 28

WHEN GOD WHISPERS YOUR NAME

He is my defender; I will not be defeated.

PSALM 62:6

*H*ere is a big question. What is God doing when you are in a bind?...
I know what we are doing. Nibbling on nails like corn on the cob. Pacing floors.
Taking pills.... But what does God do?... He fights for us. He steps into the ring
and points us to our corner and takes over. "Remain calm; the Lord will fight
for you" (Exodus 14:14). His job is to fight. Our job is to trust. Just trust.
Not direct. Or question.... Our job is to pray and wait.

SEPTEMBER 4

JUST LIKE JESUS

Come near to God, and God will come near to you.
JAMES 4:8

Some of us have tried to have a daily quiet time and have not been successful.... So rather than spend time with God, listening for his voice, we'll let others spend time with him and then benefit from their experience.... After all, isn't that why we pay preachers?... If that is your approach...I'd like to challenge you with this thought: Do you do that with other parts of your life?... [There are] certain things no one can do for you. And one of those is spending time with God.

APRIL 29

WALKING WITH THE SAVIOR

Your heart will be where your treasure is.

MATTHEW 6:21

The most powerful life is the most simple life. The most powerful life is the life that knows where it's going, that knows where the source of strength is, and the life that stays free of clutter and happenstance and hurriedness. Being busy is not a sin. Jesus was busy. Paul was busy. Peter was busy. Nothing of significance is achieved without effort and hard work and weariness.... But being busy in an endless pursuit of things that leave us empty and hollow and broken inside— that cannot be pleasing to God.

SEPTEMBER 3

THE GREAT HOUSE OF GOD

*Give us the food we need for each day. Forgive us for our sins,
just as we have forgiven those who sinned against us.*

Matthew 6:11–12

*W*e'd be wise to take seriously Paul's admonition: Why do you judge your
brothers or sisters in Christ? And why do you think you are better than they?
We will all stand before the Lord to be judged (Romans 14:10).... Your sister
would like me to remind you that she needs grace. Just like you need forgiveness,
so does she.

APRIL 30

WALKING WITH THE SAVIOR

*In Christ we are set free by the blood of his death,
and so we have forgiveness of sins.*

EPHESIANS 1:7

Jesus spoke of freedom...the type of freedom that comes not through power but through submission.... God wants to emancipate his people; he wants to set them free.... He wants them governed not by law but by love. We have been liberated from our own guilt and our own legalism. We have the freedom to pray and the freedom to love the God of our heart. And we have been forgiven by the only one who could condemn us. We are truly free!

SEPTEMBER 2

THE GREAT HOUSE OF GOD

The Lord sees the good people and listens to their prayers.
1 PETER 3:12

*Y*ou and I live in a loud world. To get someone's attention is no easy task.
He must be willing to set everything aside to listen.... When someone
is willing to silence everything else so he can hear us clearly, it is a privilege....
[Your] prayers are honored [in heaven] as precious jewels.... Your prayers
move God to change the world. You may not understand the mystery of prayer.
You don't need to. But this much is clear: Actions in heaven begin
when someone prays on earth.

MAY 1

THE APPLAUSE OF HEAVEN

Create in me a pure heart, God, and make my spirit right again.

PSALM 51:10

*W*e are thirsty. Not thirsty for fame, possessions, passion, or romance. We've drunk from those pools. They are salt water in the desert. They don't quench—they kill. "Blessed are those who hunger and thirst for righteousness...." Righteousness.... That's what we are thirsty for. We're thirsty for a clean conscience. We crave a clean slate.... We pray for a hand that will enter the dark cavern of our world and do for us the one thing we can't do for ourselves— make us right again.

SEPTEMBER 1

IN THE EYE OF THE STORM

*"Lord, if it's you," Peter says, "tell me to come
to you on the water."*

MATTHEW 14:28 NIV

Peter is not testing Jesus; he is pleading with Jesus. Stepping onto a stormy sea
is not a move of logic; it is a move of desperation.... We do the same, don't we?
We come to Christ in an hour of deep need.... We realize...that human strength
won't save us. So we look to God in desperation. We realize...that all the good
works in the world are puny when laid before the Perfect One.

MAY 2

A GENTLE THUNDER

I will make you my promised bride forever. I will be good and fair; I will show you my love and mercy.

HOSEA 2:19

The Bible has a simple story. God made man. Man rejected God. God won't give up until he wins him back. God will whisper. He will shout.... He will take away our burdens; he'll even take away our blessings. If there are a thousand steps between us and him, he will take all but one. But he will leave the final one for us. The choice is ours.

AUGUST 31

IN THE EYE OF THE STORM

Continue praying, keeping alert, and always thanking God.
COLOSSIANS 4:2

Can you imagine the outcome if a parent honored each request of each child during a trip? We'd inch our bloated bellies from one ice-cream store to the next.... Can you imagine the chaos if God indulged each of ours?... God's destiny for your life [is] salvation. God's overarching desire is that you reach that destiny.... When his sovereign plan and your earthly plan collide, a decision must be made.... If God must choose between your earthly satisfaction and your heavenly salvation, which do you hope he chooses? Me too.

MAY 3

JUST LIKE JESUS

You will be my witnesses—in Jerusalem, in all of Judea, in Samaria, and in every part of the world.

ACTS 1:8

*W*e are witnesses. And like witnesses in a court, we are called to testify, to tell what we have seen and heard. And we are to speak truthfully.... Period. There is, however, one difference between the witness in court and the witness for Christ. The witness in court eventually steps down from the witness chair, but the witness for Christ never does. Since the claims of Christ are always on trial, court is perpetually in session, and we remain under oath.

AUGUST 30

HOW TO STUDY THE BIBLE

Your word is like a lamp for my feet and a light for my path.
PSALM 119:105

*T*hough the Bible was written over sixteen centuries by at least forty authors, it has one central theme—salvation through faith in Christ. Begun by Moses in the lonely desert of Arabia and finished by John on the lonely Isle of Patmos, it is held together by a strong thread: God's passion and God's plan to save His children.... Understanding the purpose of the Bible is like setting the compass in the right direction. Calibrate it correctly and you'll journey safely.

MAY 4

WHEN CHRIST COMES

*He will change our simple bodies and make them like his
own glorious body.*

PHILIPPIANS 3:21

$\mathcal{W}$hat do we know about our resurrected bodies? They will be unlike any we
have ever imagined.... Will we still bear the scars from the pain of life?... That is
a very good question. Jesus, at least for forty days, kept his.... Peter tells us that
"by his wounds you have been healed" (1 Peter 2:24 NIV). In heaven's accounting,
only one wound is worthy to be remembered. And that is the wound of Jesus.
Our wounds will be no more.

AUGUST 29

IN THE GRIP OF GRACE

Who can accuse the people God has chosen? No one,
because God is the One who makes them right.

ROMANS 8:33

*E*very moment of your life, your accuser is filing charges against you....
Who is he? The devil.... As he speaks, you hang your head. You have no defense.
His charges are fair. "I plead guilty, your honor," you mumble. "The sentence?"
Satan asks. "The wages of sin is death," explains the judge, "but in this case the
death has already occurred. For this one died with Christ." Satan is suddenly
silent. And you are suddenly jubilant.... You have stood before the judge
and heard him declare, "Not guilty."

MAY 5

A GENTLE THUNDER

*Trust the Lord with all your heart, and don't depend
on your own understanding.*

PROVERBS 3:5

The problem with this world is that it doesn't fit. Oh, it will do for now, but it
isn't tailor-made. We were made to live with God, but on earth we live by faith.
We were made to live forever, but on this earth we live but for a moment....
We must trust God. We must trust not only that he does what is best but
that he knows what is ahead.... Trust in God, Jesus urges, and trust in me.

AUGUST 28

THE GREAT HOUSE OF GOD

God's Spirit, who is in you, is greater than the devil,
who is in the world.

1 JOHN 4:4

To the first-century church in Smyrna, Christ said, "Do not be afraid of what
you are about to suffer. I tell you, the devil will put some of you in prison to test
you, and you will suffer for ten days. But be faithful, even if you have to die,
and I will give you the crown of life" (Revelation 2:10).... Christ informs the
church of the...duration...the reason...and the outcome of the persecution....
In other words, Jesus uses Satan to fortify his church.

MAY 6

WHEN GOD WHISPERS YOUR NAME

*We proclaim him, admonishing and teaching everyone
with all wisdom, so that we may present everyone perfect
in Christ. To this end I labor, struggling with all his energy,
which so powerfully works in me.*

COLOSSIANS 1:28-29 NIV

Look at Paul's aim, to present everyone perfect in Christ.... What was his
method? Counseling and teaching. Paul's tools? Verbs. Nouns. Sentences.
Lessons. The same equipment you and I have.... Was it easier then than now?
Don't think so.... How did he do it?... He worked with all the energy he so
powerfully works in me. As Paul worked, so did God.... And as you work,
so does the Father.

AUGUST 27

IN THE GRIP OF GRACE

He gave himself for us so he might pay the price to free us from all evil and to make us pure people who belong only to him.

TITUS 2:14

*D*o we ever compromise tonight, knowing we'll confess tomorrow?... Is that the intent of grace? Is God's goal to promote disobedience? Hardly. "Grace...teaches us not to live against God nor to do the evil things the world wants us to do. Instead, that grace teaches us to live now in a wise and right way and in a way that shows we serve God" (Titus 2:11–12). God's grace has released us from selfishness. Why return?

MAY 7

WALKING WITH THE SAVIOR

You have begun to live the new life, in which you are being made new and are becoming like the One who made you.

COLOSSIANS 3:10

I wonder if Jesus doesn't muster up a slight smile as he sees his lost sheep come straggling into the fold—the beaten, broken, dirty sheep who stands at the door looking up at the Shepherd asking, "Can I come in? I don't deserve it, but...?" The Shepherd looks down at the sheep and says, "Come in, this is your home." Salvation is the process that's done...that no one can take away from you. Sanctification is the lifelong process of...growing in Christ.

AUGUST 26

IN THE GRIP OF GRACE

You will be judged in the same way that you judge others.

MATTHEW 7:2

We condemn a man for stumbling this morning, but we didn't see the blows he took yesterday. We judge a woman for the limp in her walk, but cannot see the tack in her shoe.... You don't know. Only one who has followed yesterday's steps can be their judge.... How can you dismiss a soul until God's work is complete? "God began doing a good work in you, and I am sure he will continue it until it is finished when Jesus Christ comes again" (Philippians 1:6).

MAY 8

IN THE EYE OF THE STORM

*I tell you the truth, whoever hears what I say and believes
in the One who sent me has eternal life.*

JOHN 5:24

When you recognize God as Creator, you will admire him. When you
recognize his wisdom, you will learn from him. When you discover his strength,
you will rely on him. But only when he saves you will you worship him....
Before your rescue, you could easily keep God at a distance.... Then came the
storm.... Despair fell like a fog.... In your heart, you knew there was no exit....
Suddenly you are left with one option: God.

AUGUST 25

JUST LIKE JESUS

A rule here, a rule there. A little lesson here, a little lesson there.

ISAIAH 28:10

*E*quipped with the right tools, we can learn to listen to God. What are those tools? Here are the ones I have found helpful: A regular time and place. Select a slot on your schedule and a corner of your world, and claim it for God.... A second tool you need [is] an open Bible. God speaks to us through his Word.... There is a third tool.... We also need a listening heart.... If you want to be just like Jesus, let God have you.

MAY 9

THE INSPIRATIONAL STUDY BIBLE

*The Spirit produces the fruit of love, joy, peace, patience,
kindness, goodness, faithfulness, gentleness, self-control.*

GALATIANS 5:22-23

In the third century, St. Cyprian wrote to...Donatus: This seems a cheerful
world, Donatus.... But if I climbed some great mountain and looked out...
you know very well what I would see; brigands...pirates...men murdered
to please the applauding crowds.... Yet in the midst of it, I have found a quiet
and holy people.... They are despised and persecuted, but they care not.
They have overcome the world. These people, Donatus, are Christians....
What a compliment! A quiet and holy people.... Quiet.... Not obnoxious.
Not boastful. Not demanding. Just quiet.... Holy.... Set apart.

AUGUST 24

IN THE EYE OF THE STORM

Let us come near to God with a sincere heart and a sure faith, because we have been made free from a guilty conscience.

HEBREWS 10:22

*F*aith is a desperate dive out of the sinking boat of human effort and a prayer that God will be there to pull us out of the water. The apostle Paul wrote..."For it is by grace you have been saved, through faith—and this not from yourselves, it is the gift of God—not by works, so that no one can boast" (Ephesians 2:8–9). The supreme force in salvation is God's grace.

MAY 10

IN THE EYE OF THE STORM

With one sacrifice he made perfect forever those who are being made holy.

HEBREWS 10:14

*U*nderline the word *perfect*. Note that the word is not *better*. Not *improving*. Not *on the upswing*. God doesn't improve; he perfects. He doesn't enhance; he completes.... Now I realize that there's a sense in which we're imperfect.... We still do exactly what we don't want to do. And that part of us is... "being made holy." But when it comes to our position before God, we're perfect. When he sees each of us, he sees one who has been made perfect through the One who is perfect—Jesus Christ.

AUGUST 23

WHEN CHRIST COMES

The Lord knows those who belong to him.

2 TIMOTHY 2:19

You are before the judgment seat of Christ. The book is opened and the reading begins.... But as soon as the infraction is read, grace is proclaimed.... The result? God's merciful verdict will echo through the universe.... We will stand in awe as one sin after another is proclaimed, and then pardoned.... As we see how much he has forgiven us, we will see how much he loves us. And we will worship him.... Only one is worthy of the applause of heaven, and he's the one with the pierced hands and feet.

MAY 11

IN THE GRIP OF GRACE

When I was helpless, he saved me.

PSALM 116:6

*A*s youngsters, we neighborhood kids would play street football.... The kid across the street had a dad with a great arm and a strong addiction to football.... Out of fairness he'd always ask, "Which team is losing?" Then he would join that team.... His appearance in the huddle changed the whole ball game.... You see, we not only had a new plan, we had a new leader. He brought new life to our team. God does precisely the same.... We didn't need to trade positions; we needed a new player. That player is Jesus Christ, God's firstborn Son.

AUGUST 22

IN THE GRIP OF GRACE

*I keep trying to reach the goal and get the prize
for which God called me.*

PHILIPPIANS 3:14

*B*efore Christ our lives were out of control, sloppy, and indulgent.
We didn't even know we were slobs until we met him....
Suddenly we find ourselves wanting to do good.
Go back to the old mess? Are you kidding?

MAY 12

JUST LIKE JESUS

Work as if you were doing it for the Lord, not for people.
COLOSSIANS 3:23

*W*hen do we get our first clue that [Jesus] knows he is the Son of God?
In the temple of Jerusalem.... But what does he do next?... He goes home
to his folks and learns the family business.... Want to bring focus to your life?
Do what Jesus did. Go home, love your family, and take care of business.
But Max, I want to be a missionary. Your first mission field is under your roof.
What makes you think they'll believe you overseas if they don't believe
you across the hall?

AUGUST 21

THE INSPIRATIONAL STUDY BIBLE

He said to them, "But who do you say that I am?"

MARK 8:29

*J*esus turns [to his disciples] and asks them the question. *The* question. "But who do you say that I am?"... You have been asked some important questions in your life: Will you marry me? Would you be interested in a transfer? What would you think if I told you I was pregnant? You've been asked some important questions. But the grandest of them is an anthill compared to the Everest found in the eighth chapter of Mark.

Who do you say that I am?

MAY 13

WHEN GOD WHISPERS YOUR NAME

*But grow in the grace and knowledge of our Lord
and Savior Jesus Christ.*

2 PETER 3:18 NIV

Growth is the goal of the Christian. Maturity is mandatory. If a child ceased to develop, the parent would be concerned, right?... When a Christian stops growing, help is needed.... You might be wise to get a checkup.... May I suggest one?... Why don't you check your habits?... Make these four habits regular activities and see what happens. First, the habit of prayer.... Second, the habit of study.... Third, the habit of giving.... And last of all, the habit of fellowship.

AUGUST 20

THE GREAT HOUSE OF GOD

My grace is enough for you. When you are weak,
my power is made perfect in you.

2 CORINTHIANS 12:9

There are certain mountains only God can climb.... It's not that you aren't welcome to try, it's just that you aren't able.... Mount Messiah is one mountain you weren't made to climb. Nor is Mount Self-Sufficient.... You are self-made. You...just roll up your sleeves and put in another twelve-hour day...which may be enough when it comes to making a living.... But when you face your own grave or your own guilt, your power will not do the trick.

MAY 14

THE APPLAUSE OF HEAVEN

The Lord will always lead you.

ISAIAH 58:11

*Y*ou've been there.... You've stepped away from the masses and followed the Master as he led you up the winding path to the summit.... Gently your guide invites you to sit on the rock above the tree line and look out with him at the ancient peaks that will never erode. "What is necessary is still what is sure," he confides. "Just remember: 'You'll go nowhere tomorrow that I haven't already been. Truth will still triumph.... The victory is yours....'"

AUGUST 19

THE INSPIRATIONAL STUDY BIBLE

The just shall live by faith.

ROMANS 1:16

At the moment I don't feel too smart. I just got off the wrong plane that took me to the wrong city and left me at the wrong airport.... Paul says we've all done the same thing...with our lives and God. "There is none righteous, no, not one." "All have sinned and fall short of the glory of God." We are all on the wrong plane, he says.... Every person has taken the wrong turn. And we need help.... The wrong solutions are pleasure and pride; the correct solution is Christ Jesus.

MAY 15

A GENTLE THUNDER

He will keep his agreement of love for a thousand lifetimes
for people who love him and obey his commands.

DEUTERONOMY 7:9

We are God's idea. We are his. His face. His eyes. His hands. His touch. We are him. Look deeply into the face of every human being on earth, and you will see his likeness.... We are incredibly, the body of Christ. And though we may not act like our Father, there is no greater truth than this: We are his. Unalterably. He loves us. Undyingly. Nothing can separate us from the love of Christ (see Romans 8:38–39).

AUGUST 18

A GENTLE THUNDER

I have chosen you out of the world, so you don't belong to it.
JOHN 15:19

*A*ll of us know what it is like to be in a house that is not our own.... They have beds. They have tables. They may have food and they may be warm, but they are a far cry from being "your father's house." Your father's house is where your father is.... We don't always feel welcome here on earth.... We shouldn't. This isn't our home. To feel unwelcome is no tragedy. Indeed it is healthy.

MAY 16

THE APPLAUSE OF HEAVEN

*God will show his mercy forever and ever to those
who worship and serve him.*

LUKE 1:50

God does not save us because of what we've done. Only a puny god could be
bought with tithes. Only an egotistical god would be impressed with our pain.
Only a temperamental god could be satisfied by sacrifices. Only a heartless god
would sell salvation to the highest bidders. And only a great God does for his
children what they can't do for themselves.

AUGUST 17

JUST LIKE JESUS

We are God's workers, working together.
1 CORINTHIANS 3:9

*I*t's a wonderful day indeed when we stop working for God and begin working with God.... For years I viewed God as a compassionate CEO and my role as a loyal sales representative.... Then I read 2 Corinthians 6:1: We are "God's fellow workers" (NIV).... Imagine the paradigm shift this truth creates. Rather than report to God, we work with God. Rather than check in with him and then leave, we check in with him and then follow. We are always in the presence of God.... There is never a nonsacred moment!

MAY 17

IN THE EYE OF THE STORM

God does not see the same way people see. People look at the outside of a person, but the Lord looks at the heart.

1 SAMUEL 16:7

God sees us with the eyes of a Father. He sees our defects, errors, and blemishes. But he also sees our value. What did Jesus know that enabled him to do what he did? Here's part of the answer. He knew the value of people. He knew that each human being is a treasure. And because he did, people were not a source of stress but a source of joy.

AUGUST 16

IN THE GRIP OF GRACE

It is not the healthy people who need a doctor, but the sick....
I did not come to invite good people but to invite sinners.

MATTHEW 9:12-13

God didn't look at our frazzled lives and say, "I'll die for you when you deserve it." No, despite our sin, in the face of our rebellion, he chose to adopt us.... His grace is a come-as-you-are promise from a one-of-a-kind King.... So trust your Father and claim this verse as your own: "God showed his love for us in this way: Christ died for us while we were still sinners" (Romans 5:8).

MAY 18

WHEN CHRIST COMES

You should know that your body is a temple for the Holy Spirit
who is in you. You have received the Holy Spirit from God.
So you do not belong to yourselves.

1 CORINTHIANS 6:19

You will live forever in this body. It will be different, mind you.... What is now faulty will be fixed. Your body will be different, but you won't have a different body.... God has a high regard for your body. You should as well. Respect it.... It is after all the temple of God.... You wouldn't want anyone trashing your home; God doesn't want anyone trashing his.

AUGUST 15

IN THE GRIP OF GRACE

If God is for us, who can be against us?

ROMANS 8:31 NIV

The question is not simply, "Who can be against us?" You could answer that one.... Disease, inflation, corruption, exhaustion.... But that is not the question. The question is, If GOD IS FOR US, who can be against us? God is for you. Your parents may have forgotten you, your teachers may have neglected you, your siblings may be ashamed of you; but within reach of your prayers is the maker of the oceans. God!

MAY 19

JUST LIKE JESUS

*We all have different gifts, each of which came because
of the grace God gave us.*

ROMANS 12:6

$\mathcal{T}$here are some things we want to do but simply aren't equipped
to accomplish.... Paul gives good advice in Romans 12:3: "Have a sane estimate
of your capabilities" (PHILLIPS). In other words, be aware of your strengths.
When you teach, do people listen? When you lead, do people follow?...
Where are you most productive? Identify your strengths, and then...major
in them.... Failing to focus on our strengths may prevent us from accomplishing
the unique tasks God has called us to do.

AUGUST 14

IN THE GRIP OF GRACE

So put all evil things out of your life.... These things make God angry.

COLOSSIANS 3:5-6

Many don't understand God's anger because they confuse the wrath of God with the wrath of man. The two have little in common. Human anger is typically self-driven and prone to explosions of temper and violent deeds.... It is not, however, the anger of God. God doesn't get angry because he doesn't get his way. He gets angry because disobedience always results in self-destruction. What kind of father sits by and watches his child hurt himself?

MAY 20

WHEN GOD WHISPERS YOUR NAME

When I kept things to myself, I felt weak deep inside me.

PSALM 32:3

*A*sk yourself two questions: Is there any unconfessed sin in my life?...
Whether it's too small to be mentioned or too big to be forgiven isn't yours
to decide. Your task is to be honest.... Are there any unsurrendered worries
in my heart? "Give all your worries to him, because he cares about you"
(1 Peter 5:7). The German word for worry means "to strangle." The Greek
word means "to divide the mind."... Worry is a noose on the neck and a
distraction of the mind, neither of which is befitting for joy.

AUGUST 13

WHEN GOD WHISPERS YOUR NAME

I have written your name on my hand.

ISAIAH 49:16

*M*aybe you've seen your name in some special places. On an award or diploma.... But to think that your name is on God's hand and on God's lips...my, could it be? Or perhaps you have never seen your name honored. And you can't remember when you heard it spoken with kindness. If so, it may be more difficult for you to believe that God knows your name. But he does. Written on his hand. Spoken by his mouth. Whispered by his lips. Your name.

MAY 21

A GENTLE THUNDER

Patience produces character, and character produces hope.
And this hope will never disappoint us.

ROMANS 5:4-5

*G*od is often more patient with us than we are with ourselves. We assume that if we fall, we aren't born again. If we stumble, then we aren't truly converted. If we have the old desires, then we must not be a new creation. If you are anxious about this, please remember, "God began doing a good work in you, and I am sure he will continue it until it is finished when Jesus Christ comes again" (Philippians 1:6).

AUGUST 12

IN THE EYE OF THE STORM

Our days on earth are like a shadow.

1 CHRONICLES 29:15 NIV

*H*e who "lives forever" has placed himself at the head of a band of pilgrims who mutter, "How long, O Lord? How long?" (Psalm 89:46 NIV).... Do you really want God to answer? He could, you know. He could answer in terms of the here and now with time increments we know.... But he seldom does that. He usually opts to measure the here and now against the there and then. And when you compare this life to that life, this life ain't long.

MAY 22

HE STILL MOVES STONES

*He gives strength to those who are tired and more power
to those who are weak.*

ISAIAH 40:29

*A*n example of faith was found on the wall of a concentration camp.
On it a prisoner had carved the words:
I believe in the sun, even though it doesn't shine,
I believe in love, even when it isn't shown,
I believe in God, even when he doesn't speak.
...What hand could have cut such a conviction? What eyes could have seen good
in such horror? There is only one answer: Eyes that chose to see the unseen.

AUGUST 11

IN THE GRIP OF GRACE

*May the Lord lead your hearts into God's love
and Christ's patience.*

2 THESSALONIANS 3:5

*"A*ll people will know that you are my followers if you love each other"
(John 13:35).... Could it be that unity is the key to reaching the world for
Christ?... If unity matters to God, then shouldn't unity matter to us?...
Nowhere, by the way, are we told to build unity. We are told simply to keep
unity.... How do we do that?... Does that mean we compromise our convictions?
No.... But it does mean we look long and hard at the attitudes we carry.

MAY 23

WALKING WITH THE SAVIOR

All your children will be taught by the Lord, and they will have much peace.

ISAIAH 54:13

*N*ever underestimate the power that comes when a parent pleads with God on behalf of a child. Who knows how many prayers are being answered right now because of the faithful ponderings of a parent ten or twenty years ago?... If what we are doing, in this fast-paced society, is taking us away from prayer time for our children, we're doing too much. There is nothing more special, more precious than time that a parent spends struggling and pondering with God on behalf of a child.

AUGUST 10

THE APPLAUSE OF HEAVEN

If we confess our sins, he will forgive our sins, because we can trust God to do what is right.

1 JOHN 1:9

"*If* we confess our sins...." The biggest word in Scriptures just might be that two letter one, *if*. For confessing sins—admitting failure—is exactly what prisoners of pride refuse to do.... Justification. Rationalization. Comparison.... They sound good. They sound familiar.... But in the kingdom, they sound hollow.... When you get to the point of sorrow for your sins, when you admit that you have no other option,...then cast all your cares on him for he is waiting.

MAY 24

IN THE EYE OF THE STORM

*His followers went to him and woke him, saying, "Lord, save us!
We will drown!" Jesus answered, "Why are you afraid?"*

MATTHEW 8:25-26

$\mathcal{R}$ead this verse: "Then those who were in the boat worshiped him, saying,
'Truly you are the Son of God'" (Matthew 14:33 NIV). After the storm,
[the disciples] worshiped him. They had never, as a group, done that before....
You won't find them worshiping when he heals the leper. Forgives the adulteress.
Preaches to the masses. They were willing to follow.... But only after the incident
on the sea did they worship him. Why? Simple. This time they were the
ones who were saved.

AUGUST 9

IN THE GRIP OF GRACE

I was given mercy so that in me, the worst of all sinners,
Christ Jesus could show that he has patience without limit.

1 TIMOTHY 1:16

A Union soldier was arrested on charges of desertion...[and was] sentenced
to die.... His appeal found its way to the...president [who] felt mercy for the
soldier and signed a pardon. The soldier returned to service...and was killed
in the last battle. Found within his breast pocket...close to the heart of the soldier
were his leader's words of pardon. He found courage in grace. I wonder how
many thousands more have found courage in the emblazoned cross of their
heavenly king.

MAY 25

WHEN CHRIST COMES

*When Jesus was raised from the dead it was a signal
of the end of death-as-the-end.*

ROMANS 6:5-6 THE MESSAGE

The resurrection is an exploding flare announcing to all sincere seekers that it is safe to believe. Safe to believe in ultimate justice. Safe to believe in eternal bodies. Safe to believe in heaven as our estate.... Safe to believe in a time when questions won't keep us awake and pain won't keep us down. Safe to believe in open graves and endless days and genuine praise. Because we can accept the resurrection story, it is safe to accept the rest of the story.

AUGUST 8

HE STILL MOVES STONES

The Lord is close to the brokenhearted, and he saves those whose spirits have been crushed.

PSALM 34:18

"*E*verything that was written in the past was written to teach us," (Romans 15:4).... These are not just Sunday school stories. Not romantic fables.... They are historical moments in which a real God met real pain so we could answer the question, "Where is God when I hurt?"... The God who spoke still speaks.... The God who came still comes. He comes into our world. He comes into your world. He comes to do what you can't.

MAY 26

THE INSPIRATIONAL STUDY BIBLE

Your kingdom is built on what is right and fair.
Love and truth are in all you do.

PSALM 89:14

*T*he single most difficult pursuit is truth and love. That sentence is grammatically correct. I know every English teacher would like to pluralize it to read: The most difficult pursuits are those of truth and love. But that's not what I mean to say.... Pursue truth and love at the same time and...you're in for the ride of your life. Love in truth. Truth in love. Never one at the expense of the other.... To pursue both is our singular task.

AUGUST 7

JUST LIKE JESUS

As a deer thirsts for streams of water, so I thirst for you, God.
PSALM 42:1

Jesus didn't act unless he saw his father act. He didn't judge until he heard his father judge. No act or deed occurred without his father's guidance.... Because Jesus could hear what others couldn't, he acted differently than they did.... Remember when everyone was distraught about Lazarus's illness? Jesus wasn't.... It was as if Jesus could hear what no one else could.... Jesus had unbroken communion with his father. Do you suppose the Father desires the same for us? Absolutely!

MAY 27

WHEN GOD WHISPERS YOUR NAME

Fix your attention on God. You'll be changed from the inside out.

ROMANS 12:2 THE MESSAGE

Real change is an inside job.... Allow me to get specific. Our problem is sin.
Not finances. Not budgets.... We are in rebellion against our Creator.
We are separated from our Father. We are cut off from the source of life....
That's why the Bible uses drastic terms like conversion, repentance,
and lost and found. Society may renovate, but only God re-creates.

AUGUST 6

WHEN GOD WHISPERS YOUR NAME

God began doing a good work in you, and I am sure he will continue it until it is finished when Jesus Christ comes again.

PHILIPPIANS 1:6

*G*od is not finished with you yet. Oh, you may think he is. You may think you've peaked. You may think he's got someone else to do the job. If so, think again.... Did you see what God is doing? A good work in you. Did you see when he will be finished? When Jesus comes again. May I spell out the message? God ain't finished with you yet.

MAY 28

JUST LIKE JESUS

Enjoy serving the Lord, and he will give you what you want.

PSALM 37:4

When we submit to God's plans, we can trust our desires. Our assignment is found at the intersection of God's plan and our pleasures.... Each of us has been made to serve God in a unique way.... The longings of your heart, then, are not incidental; they are critical messages. The desires of your heart are not to be ignored; they are to be consulted. As the wind turns the weather vane, so God uses your passions to turn your life. God is too gracious to ask you to do something you hate.

AUGUST 5

WHEN CHRIST COMES

Many of those who sleep in the dust of the earth shall awake, some to everlasting life, and some to shame and everlasting contempt.

DANIEL 12:2 RSV

*D*oes hell serve a purpose?... Remove it from the Bible and, at the same time, remove any notion of a just God and a trustworthy Scripture.... If there is no hell, God is blind toward the victims and has turned his back on those who pray for relief. If there is no wrath toward evil, then God is not love, for love hates that which is evil.... The Bible repeatedly and stoutly affirms...some will be saved. Some will be lost.

MAY 29

WHEN CHRIST COMES

As a man rejoices over his new wife, so your God will rejoice over you.

ISAIAH 62:5

*H*ave you ever noticed the way a groom looks at his bride during the wedding? I have.... If the light is just so...I can see a tiny reflection in his eyes. Her reflection. And the sight of her reminds him why he is here.... And such are precisely the feelings of Jesus. Look long enough into the eyes of our Savior and, there, too, you will see a bride.... And who is this bride for whom Jesus longs?... You are. You have captured the heart of God.

AUGUST 4

IN THE EYE OF THE STORM

He felt sorry for them and healed those who were sick.

MATTHEW 14:14

$\mathcal{M}$atthew writes that Jesus "healed their sick." Not some of their sick. Not the righteous among the sick.... But "the sick." Surely, among the many thousands, there were a few people unworthy of good health. The same divinity that gave Jesus the power to heal also gave him the power to perceive.... Undoubtedly, there were those in the multitude who would use their newfound health to hurt others.... Each time Jesus healed, he had to overlook the future and the past. Something, by the way, that he still does.

MAY 30

THE APPLAUSE OF HEAVEN

Since God has shown us great mercy, I beg you to offer your lives as a living sacrifice to him.

ROMANS 12:1

There is a dangerous point at which anger ceases to be an emotion and becomes a driving force. A person bent on revenge moves unknowingly further and further away from being able to forgive, for to be without the anger is to be without a source of energy.... Revenge is the raging fire that consumes the arsonist. Bitterness is the trap that snares the hunter. And mercy is the choice that can set them all free.

AUGUST 3

THE APPLAUSE OF HEAVEN

*I praise you because you made me in an amazing
and wonderful way.*

PSALM 139:14

Stradivarius has become synonymous with excellence. He once said that
to make a violin less than his best would be to rob God, who could not make
Antonio Stradivari's violins without Antonio. He was right.... Certain gifts were
given to that craftsman that no other violin maker possessed. In the same vein,
there are certain things you can do that no one else can.... You have an
instrument and a song, and you owe it to God to play them both sublimely.

MAY 31

THE APPLAUSE OF HEAVEN

He restores my soul; He leads me in the paths of righteousness for His name's sake.

PSALM 23:3 NKJV

It's hard to see things grow old.... I wish I could make it all new again...
but I can't. I can't. But God can. "He restores my soul," wrote the shepherd.
He doesn't reform; he restores. He doesn't camouflage the old; he restores
the new. The Master Builder will pull out the original plan and restore it.
He will restore the vigor. He will restore the energy. He will restore the hope.
He will restore the soul.

AUGUST 2

AND THE ANGELS WERE SILENT

Jesus said, "Come follow me."
MATTHEW 4:19

God is an inviting God. He invited Mary to birth his Son, the disciples to fish for men, the adulteress woman to start over, and Thomas to touch his wounds. God is the King who prepares the palace, sets the table, and invites his subjects to come in. In fact, it seems his favorite word is *come....* "All you who are thirsty, come and drink." "Come to me all, all of you who are tired and have heavy loads, and I will give you rest."

JUNE 1

WHEN GOD WHISPERS YOUR NAME

We brought nothing into the world, so we can take nothing out.
But, if we have food and clothes, we will be satisfied with that.

1 TIMOTHY 6:7-8

*A*s a child we say, "If only I were a teenager." As a teen we say, "If only I were an adult," As an adult, "If only I were married."... We are not satisfied. Contentment is a difficult virtue. Why? Because there is nothing on earth that can satisfy our deepest longing. We long to see God. The leaves of life are rustling with the rumor that we will—and we won't be satisfied until we do.

AUGUST 1

JUST LIKE JESUS

Remain in me, and I will remain in you. A branch cannot produce fruit alone but must remain in the vine.

JOHN 15:4

God wants to be as close to us as a branch is to a vine.... God also uses the temple to depict the intimacy he desires. "Don't you know," Paul writes, "that your body is the temple of the Holy Spirit, who lives in you and was given to you by God?" (1 Corinthians 6:19 TEV)... God didn't come and go, appear and disappear [from the temple]. He was a permanent presence, always available. What incredibly good news for us! We are NEVER away from God!

JUNE 2

WHEN CHRIST COMES

Christ rose first; then when Christ comes back,
all his people will become alive again.

1 CORINTHIANS 15:23 TLB

God has made [a] promise to us. "I will come back...," he assures us.
Yes, the rocks will tumble. Yes, the ground will shake. But the child of God
needn't fear—for the Father has promised to take us to be with him.
But...isn't there a cautious part of us that wonders how reliable these words
may be?... How can we know he will do what he said?... Because he's already
done it once.

JULY 31

WHEN GOD WHISPERS YOUR NAME

I have learned the secret of being happy at any time
in everything that happens.

PHILIPPIANS 4:12

*P*eer into the prison and see [Paul] for yourself: bent and frail, shackled to the arm of a Roman guard. Behold the apostle of God.... He introduced himself as the worst sinner in history.... "What a miserable man I am! Who will save me from this body that brings me death?" (Romans 7:24). Only heaven knows how long he stared at the question before he found the courage to defy logic and write, "I thank God for saving me through Jesus Christ our Lord!" (Romans 7:25).

JUNE 3

WHEN GOD WHISPERS YOUR NAME

*The teaching I ask you to accept is easy;
the load I give you to carry is light.*

MATTHEW 11:30

If you are at peace with yourself—if you like yourself—
you will get along with others.
The converse is also true. If you don't like yourself, if you are
ashamed, embarrassed, or angry, other people are going to know it....
Which takes us to the question, "How does a person get relief?"...
"Come to me, all of you who are tired and have heavy loads, and I will give
you rest" (Matthew 11:28).... Jesus says he is the solution for weariness of soul.

JULY 30

THE APPLAUSE OF HEAVEN

The wisdom of this world is foolishness with God.

1 CORINTHIANS 3:19

[Power] comes in many forms.... And all have the same goal: "I will get what I want at your expense." And all have the same end: futility.... Absolute power is unreachable.... When you stand at the top—if there is a top—the only way to go is down. And the descent is often painful.... A thousand years from now, will it matter what title the world gave you? No, but it will make a literal hell of a difference whose child you are.

JUNE 4

THE APPLAUSE OF HEAVEN

*I am the Lord your God, who holds your right hand,
and I tell you, "Don't be afraid. I will help you."*

ISAIAH 41:13

*W*e need to remember that the disciples were common men given a
compelling task. Before they were the stained-glassed saints in the windows
of cathedrals, they were somebody's next-door-neighbors trying to make a
living and raise a family. They weren't cut from theological cloth or raised
on supernatural milk. But they were an ounce more devoted than they were
afraid and, as a result, did some extraordinary things.

JULY 29

IN THE EYE OF THE STORM

*Through his power all things were made—things in heaven
and on earth, things seen and unseen.*

COLOSSIANS 1:16

*W*ith one decision, history began. Existence became measurable.... And on this earth? A mighty hand went to work.... Look to the canyons to see the Creator's splendor. Touch the flowers and see his delicacy. Listen to the thunder and hear his power.... Today you will encounter God's creation. When you see the beauty around you, let each detail remind you to lift your head in praise. Express your appreciation for God's creation. Encourage others to see the beauty of his creation.

JUNE 5

WHEN CHRIST COMES

Don't let your hearts be troubled. Trust in God, and trust in me.
There are many rooms in my Father's house; I would not tell
you this it if were not true. I am going there to prepare a place
for you.... I will come back and take you to be with me so that
you may be where I am going.

JOHN 14:1-3

*R*educe the [above] paragraph to a sentence and it might read:
"You do the trusting and I'll do the taking."

JULY 28

HE STILL MOVES STONES

Even when you are old, I will be the same. Even when your hair has turned gray, I will take care of you.

ISAIAH 46:4

Growing old can be dangerous. The trail is treacherous and the pitfalls are many. One is wise to be prepared. You know it's coming.... If growing old catches you by surprise, don't blame God. He gave you plenty of warning. He also gave you plenty of advice. Your last chapters can be your best.... It could be that all of your life has prepared you for a grand exit. God's oldest have always been among his choicest.

JUNE 6

JUST LIKE JESUS

He came to serve others and to give his life as a ransom for many people.

MARK 10:45

One of the incredible abilities of Jesus was to stay on target.... As Jesus looked across the horizon of his future, he could see many targets.... But in the end he chose to be a Savior and save souls.... "The Son of Man came to find lost people and save them" (Luke 19:10).... The heart of Christ was relentlessly focused on one task. The day he left the carpentry shop of Nazareth he had one ultimate aim—the cross of Calvary.

JULY 27

IN THE EYE OF THE STORM

What we see will last only a short time, but what we cannot see will last forever.

2 CORINTHIANS 4:18

For some of you, the journey has been long. Very long and stormy. In no way do I wish to minimize the difficulties that you have had to face along the way.... And you are tired.... You want to go on, but some days the road seems so long.... Let me encourage you.... God never said that the journey would be easy, but he did say that the arrival would be worthwhile.

JUNE 7

IN THE GRIP OF GRACE

Get along with each other, and forgive each other. If someone does wrong to you, forgive that person because the Lord forgave you.

COLOSSIANS 3:13

*U*nity doesn't begin in examining others but in examining self. Unity begins not in demanding that others change, but in admitting that we aren't so perfect ourselves.... The answer to arguments? Acceptance. The first step to unity? Acceptance. Not agreement, acceptance. Not unanimity, acceptance. Not negotiation, arbitration, or elaboration. Those might come later but only after the first step, acceptance.

JULY 26

A GENTLE THUNDER

Anyone who wants to be a friend of the world becomes God's enemy.

JAMES 4:4

*J*ohn the Baptist...was a public relations disaster.... His message was as rough as his dress: a no-nonsense, bare-fisted challenge to repent because God was on his way. John the Baptist set himself apart for one task, to be a voice of Christ.... You don't have to be like the world to have an impact on the world.... You don't have to lower yourself down to their level to lift them up to your level. Holiness doesn't seek to be odd. Holiness seeks to be like God.

JUNE 8

THE GREAT HOUSE OF GOD

God can do all things.

MATTHEW 19:26

You want to know who God is?... Take a look at his creation.... He is untainted
by the atmosphere of sin, unbridled by the time line of history, unhindered
by the weariness of the body. What controls you doesn't control him.... Is an
eagle disturbed by traffic? No, he rises above it. Is the whale perturbed by a
hurricane? Of course not, he plunges beneath it. Is the lion flustered by the
mouse standing directly in his way? No, he steps over it. How much more is
God able to soar above, plunge beneath, and step over the troubles of the earth!

JULY 25

WHEN CHRIST COMES

We all have wandered away like sheep; each of us has gone his own way.

ISAIAH 53:6

How could a loving God send people to hell?... God does not "send" people to hell. Nor does he send "people" to hell.... The word "people" is neutral, implying innocence. Nowhere does Scripture teach that innocent people are condemned. People do not go to hell. Sinners do. The rebellious do. The self-centered do. So how could a loving God send people to hell? He doesn't. He simply honors the choice of sinners.

JUNE 9

WALKING WITH THE SAVIOR

To the King that rules forever, who will never die, who cannot be seen, the only God, be honor and glory forever and ever.

1 TIMOTHY 1:17

The whole purpose of coming before the King is to praise him, to live in recognition of his splendor. Praise...is the occupation of those who dwell in the kingdom. Praise is the highest occupation of any being. What happens when we praise the Father? We reestablish the proper chain of command; we recognize that the King is on the throne and that he has saved his people.

JULY 24

WHEN GOD WHISPERS YOUR NAME

*They continue saying things that mean nothing, thinking
that God will hear them because of their many words.*

MATTHEW 6:7

I love the short sentence.... Keep the ones you like.
Forgive the ones you don't. Share them when you can.
Pray all the time. If necessary, use words....
Greed I've often regretted. Generosity—never....
No one is useless to God. No one.
Nails didn't hold God to a cross. Love did.
You will never forgive anyone more than God has already forgiven you.

JUNE 10

IN THE EYE OF THE STORM

Honor God and obey his commands, because this is all people must do.

ECCLESIASTES 12:13

*H*ere are some God-given, time-tested truths that define the way you should navigate your life.... Love God more than you fear hell. Make major decisions in a cemetery. When no one is watching, live as if someone is. Succeed at home first. Don't spend tomorrow's money today. Pray twice as much as you fret. God has forgiven you; you'd be wise to do the same.

JULY 23

HE STILL MOVES STONES

Give all your worries to him, because he cares about you.
1 PETER 5:7

*W*orry...makes you forget who's in charge. And when the focus is on yourself...you worry. You become anxious about many things.... With time, your agenda becomes more important than God's. You're more concerned with presenting self than pleasing him. And you may even find yourself doubting God's judgment.... God has gifted you with talents. He has done the same to your neighbor. If you concern yourself with your neighbor's talents, you will neglect yours. But if you concern yourself with yours, you could inspire both.

JUNE 11

WHEN GOD WHISPERS YOUR NAME

So now you are not a slave; you are God's child, and God will give you the blessing he promised.

GALATIANS 4:7

*D*o you rise above the past and make a difference? Or do you remain controlled by the past and make excuses?... Many choose the convalescent homes of the heart.... Back and forth they rock in the chair of regret.... Lean closely and you will hear them: "If only."... Maybe you've used those words.... If such is the case... go to John's gospel and read Jesus' words: "Human life comes from human parents, but spiritual life comes from the Spirit" (John 3:6).

JULY 22

JUST LIKE JESUS

You were taught to be made new in your hearts, to become a new person.... Made to be like God—made to be truly good and holy.

EPHESIANS 4:23-24

*H*ealthy marriages have a...tenderness, an honesty, an on-going communication. The same is true in our relationship with God. Sometimes we go to him with our joys, and sometimes we go with our hurts, but we always go. And as we go, the more we go, the more we become like him.... People who live long lives together eventually begin to [become] alike. As we walk with God...we take on his heart.

JUNE 12

A GENTLE THUNDER

Come back to the Lord your God, because he is kind and shows mercy. He doesn't become angry quickly, and he has great love.

JOEL 2:13

*H*ow far do you want God to go in getting your attention? If God has to choose between your eternal safety and your earthly comfort, which do you hope he chooses? What if he moved you to another land? (As he did Abraham.) What if he called you out of retirement? (Remember Moses?).... God does what it takes to get our attention. Isn't that the message of the Bible? The relentless pursuit of God.

JULY 21

THE APPLAUSE OF HEAVEN

I saw the holy city, the New Jerusalem, coming down out of heaven from God. It was prepared like a bride dressed for her husband.

REVELATION 21:2

*W*hat is more beautiful than a bride?... Maybe it is the aura of whiteness that clings to her as dew clings to a rose. Or perhaps it is the diamonds that glisten in her eyes.... A commitment robed in elegance.... Tomorrow bringing hope today. Promised purity faithfully delivered. When you read that our heavenly home is similar to a bride, tell me, doesn't it make you want to go home?

JUNE 13

WHEN CHRIST COMES

*Now we see a dim reflection, as if we were looking into a mirror,
but then we shall see clearly.*

1 CORINTHIANS 13:12

What will happen when you see Jesus? You will see unblemished purity
and unbending strength. You will feel his unending presence and know his
unbridled protection. And—all that he is, you will be, for you will be like Jesus....
Since you'll be pure as snow, you will never sin again;...you will never stumble
again;...you will never feel lonely again.... When Christ comes, you will dwell
in the light of God. And you will see him as he really is.

JULY 20

HE STILL MOVES STONES

*I am the Lord, the God of every person on the earth.
Nothing is impossible for me.*

JEREMIAH 32:27

We need to hear that God is still in control.... We need to hear that life's mishaps and tragedies are not a reason to bail out. They are simply a reason to sit tight. Corrie ten Boom used to say, "When the train goes through a tunnel and the world gets dark, do you jump out? Of course not. You sit still and trust the engineer to get you through."... Go back and read the story of God.... You aren't the first person to be helped.

JUNE 14

A GENTLE THUNDER

If we say we have no sin, we are fooling ourselves,
and the truth is not in us.

1 JOHN 1:8

My daughter Andrea got a splinter in her finger. I took her to the restroom and set out some tweezers, ointment, and a Band-Aid. She didn't like what she saw. "I just want the Band-Aid, Daddy." Sometimes we are just like Andrea. We come to Christ with our sin, but all we want is a covering.... And one wonders if God, even in his great mercy, will heal what we conceal.... How can God touch what we cover up?

JULY 19

AND THE ANGELS WERE SILENT

*If you don't want to serve the Lord, you must choose
for yourselves today whom you will serve.*

JOSHUA 24:15

Isn't it incredible that God leaves the choice to us? Think about it.
There are many things in life we can't choose.... We can't control the economy.
We can't choose whether or not we are born with a big nose or blue eyes or a
lot of hair. We can't even choose how people respond to us. But we can choose
where we spend eternity. The big choice, God leaves to us.... That is the
only decision which really matters.

JUNE 15

HE STILL MOVES STONES

He took our suffering on him and carried our diseases.

MATTHEW 8:17

*P*icture a battleground strewn with wounded bodies, and you see Bethesda.
Imagine a nursing home overcrowded and understaffed, and you see the pool.
Call to mind the orphans in Bangladesh or the abandoned in New Delhi,
and you will see what people saw when they passed Bethesda. As they passed,
what...did they do? Most walked past.... But not Jesus.... He is alone....
The people need him—so he's there. Can you picture it? Jesus walking
among the suffering.

JULY 18

IN THE EYE OF THE STORM

All have sinned and are not good enough for God's glory, and all need to be made right with God by his grace, which is a free gift.

ROMANS 3:23-24

The supreme force in salvation is God's grace. Not our works.... Salvation is God's sudden, calming presence during the stormy seas of our lives. We hear his voice; we take the step.... So we...leave behind the Titanic of self-righteousness and stand on the solid path of God's grace. And, surprisingly, we are able to walk on water.... And God is not only within sight, he is within reach.

JUNE 16

THE GREAT HOUSE OF GOD

The Lord himself will go before you. He will be with you;
he will not leave you or forget you.

DEUTERONOMY 31:8

When I was seven years old, I ran away from home. I'd had enough
of my father's rules.... I didn't go far.... I was hungry, so I went back home.
Though the rebellion was brief, it was rebellion nonetheless.... I didn't get a
robe and a ring and sandals like the prodigal did. But I learned from my father
[that]...our God is no fair-weather Father.... I can count on him to be
in my corner no matter how I perform. You can, too.

JULY 17

WHEN GOD WHISPERS YOUR NAME

Don't get angry. Don't be upset; it only leads to trouble.

PSALM 37:8

*A*nger. It's easy to define: the noise of the soul. Anger. The unseen irritant of the heart.... X-ray the world of the vengeful and behold the tumor of bitterness: black, menacing, malignant. Carcinoma of the spirit. Its fatal fibers creep around the edge of the heart and ravage it. Yesterday you can't alter, but your reaction to yesterday you can. The past you cannot change, but your response to your past you can.

JUNE 17

NO WONDER THEY CALL HIM THE SAVIOR

If they could be made God's people by what they did,
God's gift of grace would not really be a gift.

ROMANS 11:6

To whom does God offer his gift? To the brightest? The most beautiful...? No.
His gift is for us all.... And he wants us so badly, he'll take us in any condition—
"as is" reads the tag on our collars. He's not about to wait for us to reach
perfection (he knows we'll never get there!).... Remember, Christ died for us
when we were still sinners. His sacrifice, then, was not dependent
on our performance. He wants us now.

JULY 16

WHEN GOD WHISPERS YOUR NAME

"Lord, how many times shall I forgive my brother when he sins against me?" Jesus answered, "...seventy-seven times."

MATTHEW 18:21-22 NIV

Seems to me God gives a lot more grace than we'd ever imagine. We could do the same. I'm not for watering down the truth or compromising the gospel. But if a fellow with a pure heart calls God Father, can't I call that same man Brother?... If God can tolerate my mistakes, can't I tolerate the mistakes of others?... If God allows me with my foibles and failures to call him Father, shouldn't I extend the same grace to others?

JUNE 18

WHEN GOD WHISPERS YOUR NAME

Faith means being sure of the things we hope for and knowing that something is real even if we do not see it.

HEBREWS 11:1

Faith is trusting what the eye can't see. Eyes see the prowling lion. Faith sees Daniel's angel. Eyes see storms. Faith sees Noah's rainbow.... Your eyes look in the mirror and see a sinner, a failure, a promise-breaker. But by faith you look in the mirror and see a robed prodigal bearing the ring of grace on your finger and the kiss of your Father on your face.

JULY 15

JUST LIKE JESUS

Pray in the Spirit at all times with all kinds of prayers,
asking for everything you need.

EPHESIANS 6:18

*H*ow do I live in God's presence? How do I detect his unseen hand
on my shoulder and his inaudible voice in my ear?... How can you and I grow
familiar with the voice of God? Here are a few ideas:... Before you step out
of bed, step into his presence.... Spend time with him in silence.... [Consider]
every moment as a potential time of communion with God.... Conclude
the day as you began it: talking to God.

JUNE 19

IN THE GRIP OF GRACE

Before I made you in your mother's womb, I chose you.

JEREMIAH 1:5

With God in your world, you aren't an accident or an incident; you are a gift to the world, a divine work of art, signed by God. One of the finest gifts I ever received is a football signed by thirty former professional quarterbacks. There is nothing unique about this ball.... What makes it unique is the signatures. The same is true with us. In the scheme of nature Homo sapiens are not unique.... What makes us special is not only our body but the signature of God on our lives.

JULY 14

THE APPLAUSE OF HEAVEN

Go back and report to John what you hear and see:
The blind receive sight, the lame walk...and the good
news is preached to the poor.

MATTHEW 11:4

This was Jesus' answer to John's agonized query...: "Are you the one who was
to come, or should we expect someone else?" I like to think of a slight smile
coming over his lips as he heard what his Master said. For now he understood.
It wasn't that Jesus was silent; it was that...John had been listening for an answer
to his earthly problems, while Jesus was busy resolving his heavenly ones.

JUNE 20

THE GREAT HOUSE OF GOD

Those who see the Son and believe in him have eternal life....
This is what my Father wants.

JOHN 6:40

We learn God's will by spending time in his presence. The key to knowing
God's heart is having a relationship with him.... God will speak to you differently
than he will speak to others.... For that reason, your walk with God is essential.
His heart is not seen in an occasional chat or weekly visit. We learn his will as
we take up residence in his house every single day.... Walk with him long
enough and you come to know his heart.

JULY 13

AND THE ANGELS WERE SILENT

*This is what the Lord God says: I, myself, will search
for my sheep and take care of them.*

EZEKIEL 34:11

*H*e's waiting for you. God is standing on the porch of heaven, expectantly
hoping, searching the horizon for a glimpse of his child. You're the one God is
seeking. God is the waiting Father, the caring Shepherd in search of his lamb....
The message is simple: God gave up his Son in order to rescue all his sons
and daughters. To bring his children home. He's listening for your answer.

JUNE 21

WALKING WITH THE SAVIOR

Perhaps you do not understand that God is kind to you so you will change your hearts and lives.

ROMANS 2:4

No one is happier than the one who has sincerely repented of wrong. Repentance is the decision to turn from selfish desires and seek God. It is a genuine, sincere regret that creates sorrow and moves us to admit wrong and desire to do better. It's an inward conviction that expresses itself in outward actions. You look at the love of God and you can't believe he's loved you like he has, and this realization motivates you to change your life.

JULY 12

IN THE EYE OF THE STORM

Jesus went to them, walking on the sea....
And they cried out in fear.

MATTHEW 14:25-26 NKJV

*E*very so often a storm will come, and I'll look up...and say, "God, a little light please?" The light came for the disciples. A figure came to them walking on the water. It wasn't what they expected.... And since Jesus came in a way they didn't expect, they almost missed seeing the answer to their prayers. And unless we look and listen closely, we risk making the same mistake. God's lights in our dark nights are as numerous as the stars, if only we'll look for them.

JUNE 22

JUST LIKE JESUS

Holy, holy, holy is the Lord God Almighty. He was, he is, and he is coming.

REVELATION 4:8

*E*xactly what is worship?... Worship is the act of magnifying God. Enlarging our vision of him.... Of course, his size doesn't change, but our perception of him does. As we draw nearer, he seems larger. Isn't that what we need? A big view of God? Don't we have big problems, big worries, big questions? Of course we do. Hence we need a big view of God. Worship offers that. How can we sing, "Holy, Holy, Holy" and not have our vision expanded?

JULY 11

WALKING WITH THE SAVIOR

Be sure that no one pays back wrong for wrong, but always try to do what is good for each other and for all people.

1 THESSALONIANS 5:15

*J*esus described for his followers what he came to do. He came to build a relationship with people. He came to take away enmity, to take away the strife, to take away the isolation that existed between God and man. Once he bridged that, once he overcame that, he said, "I will call you friends."

JUNE 23

IN THE GRIP OF GRACE

*Love the Lord your God with all your heart, all your soul,
and all your mind.*

MATTHEW 22:37

𝓜ine deep enough in every heart and you'll find it: a longing for meaning,
a quest for purpose.... Some search for meaning in a career.... They opt to be a
human "doing" rather than a human "being".... For others, who they are is what
they have. They...are always seeking meaning in something they own....
All mirages in the desert of purpose....
Shouldn't we face the truth? If we don't acknowledge God,
we are flotsam in the universe.

JULY 10

WHEN CHRIST COMES

Don't be afraid of people, who can kill the body but cannot kill the soul. The only one you should fear is the one who can destroy the soul and the body in hell.

MATTHEW 10:28

*H*ell's misery is deep, but not as deep as God's love. So how do we apply this [truth]? If you are saved, it should cause you to rejoice. You've been rescued. A glance into hell leads the believer to rejoice. But it also leads the believer to redouble his efforts to reach the lost. To understand hell is to pray more earnestly and to serve more diligently. Ours is a high-stakes mission.

JUNE 24

A GENTLE THUNDER

God is being patient with you.... He wants all people
to change their hearts and lives.

2 PETER 3:9

[To those who embrace Christ as Savior,] he has promised a new birth....
Does that mean you will instantly be able to resist any temptation?
To answer that question, compare your new birth in Christ to a newborn baby.
Can a newborn walk?... No, not yet. But someday he will. It takes time to grow.
But is the parent in the delivery room ashamed of the baby?... Of course
not...they are proud. They know that growth will come with time. So does God.

JULY 9

WHEN GOD WHISPERS YOUR NAME

Life is not measured by how much one owns.

LUKE 12:15

Jesus had a definition for greed. He called it the practice of measuring life
by possessions. Greed equates a person's worth with a person's purse....
The consequence of such a philosophy is predictable. If you are the sum of what
you own, then by all means own it all. No price is too high. No payment is too
much.... Greed is not defined by what something costs; it is measured by what it
costs you. If anything costs you your faith or your family, the price is too high.

JUNE 25

WHEN GOD WHISPERS YOUR NAME

Continue to have faith and do what you know is right. Some people have rejected this, and their faith has been shipwrecked.

1 TIMOTHY 1:19

I sit a few feet from a man on death row.... I'm curious about what bolsters this man as he nears his execution. So I ask some questions.

Do you have family, Paul? I have none.

What about your health? My body is beaten and tired....

Then what do you have, Paul?... What do you have that matters?

I have my faith. It's all I have. But it's all I need.

JULY 8

A GENTLE THUNDER

God is strong and can help you not to fall.
JUDE 24

You and I are on a great climb.... You took your first step the day you confessed Christ as the Son of God. He gave you his harness—the Holy Spirit. In your hands he placed a rope—his Word. Your first steps were confident and strong, but with the journey came weariness, and with the height came fear. You lost your footing.... For a moment, which seemed like forever, you tumbled wildly.... But then the rope tightened, and the tumble ceased.... And though you can't see your guide, you know him. You know he is strong. You know he is able to keep you from falling.

JUNE 26

IN THE EYE OF THE STORM

Jesus spoke to them, saying, "Be of good cheer! It is I;
do not be afraid."

MATTHEW 14:27 NKJV

*W*hen the disciples saw Jesus in the middle of their stormy night, they called him a ghost.... To them, the glow was anything but God.... We often have the same reaction. We dismiss occasional kindness as apparitions, accidents, or anomalies. Anything but God.... And because we look for the bonfire, we miss the candle. Because we listen for the shout, we miss the whisper. But it is in burnished candles that God comes, and through whispered promises he speaks.

JULY 7

JUST LIKE JESUS

Our faces, then, are not covered. We all show the Lord's glory,
and we are being changed to be like him.

2 CORINTHIANS 3:18

The purpose of worship is to change the face of the worshiper....
The connection between the face and worship is more than coincidental.
Our face is the most public part of our bodies, covered less than any other area.
It is also the most recognizable part.... God desires to take our faces, this exposed
and memorable part of our bodies, and use them to reflect his goodness.

JUNE 27

WHEN CHRIST COMES

On the day when the Lord Jesus comes,...all the people who have believed will be amazed at Jesus.

2 THESSALONIANS 1:10

*W*hen we see Christ,...we will see the perfect priest.... A priest presents people to God and God to people. You have known other priests...whether clergy or not, who sought to bring you to God. But they, too, needed a priest.... They, like you, were sinful. Not so with Jesus. "Jesus is the kind of high priest we need. He is holy, sinless, pure, not influenced by sinners, and he is raised above the heavens" (Hebrews 7:26). Jesus is the perfect priest.

JULY 6

WALKING WITH THE SAVIOR

*If you suffer for doing good, and you are patient,
then God is pleased.*

1 PETER 2:20

*I*s there any emotion that imprisons the soul more than the unwillingness
to forgive? What do you do when people mistreat you or those you love?
Does the fire of anger boil within you...? Or do you reach somewhere, to some
source of cool water and pull out a bucket of mercy—to free yourself?
Don't get on the roller coaster of resentment and anger. You be the one
who says, "Yes, he mistreated me, but I am going to be like Christ."

JUNE 28

HE STILL MOVES STONES

If you forgive others for their sins, your Father in heaven will also forgive you for your sins.

MATTHEW 6:14

*B*itterness is its own prison.... The dungeon, deep and dark, is beckoning you to enter.... You can choose, like many, to chain yourself to your hurt.... Or you can choose, like some, to put away your hurts before they become hates.... How does God deal with your bitter heart? He reminds you that what you have is more important than what you don't have. You still have your relationship with God. No one can take that.

JULY 5

IN THE EYE OF THE STORM

Be holy in all you do, just as God, the One who called you, is holy.

1 PETER 1:15

I have something against the lying voices that noise our world. You've heard them. They tell you to swap your integrity for a new sale. To barter your convictions for an easy deal. To exchange your devotion for a quick thrill. They whisper. They woo. They taunt. They tantalize. They flirt. They flatter.... The world rams at your door; Jesus taps at your door. The voices scream for your allegiance; Jesus softly and tenderly requests it. The world promises flashy pleasure; Jesus promises a quiet dinner...with God.
Which voice do you hear?

JUNE 29

WHEN GOD WHISPERS YOUR NAME

You gave me life and showed me kindness, and in your care you watched over my life.

JOB 10:12

*D*iscipline is easy for me to swallow. Logical to assimilate. Manageable and appropriate. But God's grace? Anything but. Examples?... Peter denied Christ before he preached Christ. Zacchaeus, the crook.... The thief on the cross.... Story after story. Prayer after prayer.... Seems that God is looking more for ways to get us home than for ways to keep us out. I challenge you to find one soul who came to God seeking grace and did not find it.

JULY 4

A GENTLE THUNDER

Those who believe in the Son have eternal life, but those who do not obey the Son will never have life.

JOHN 3:36

When does salvation come? When we look to Christ. When we embrace him as Savior. Astonishingly simple, isn't it?... And for those who believe, he has promised a new birth. But despite the simplicity, there are still those who don't believe. They don't trust the promise.... If only they would try. If only they would test it. But God is as polite as he is passionate. He never forces his way in. The choice is theirs.

JUNE 30

JUST LIKE JESUS

He put a new song in my mouth, a song of praise to our God.

PSALM 40:3

God invites us to see his face so he can change ours. He uses our uncovered faces to display his glory.... By his fingers, wrinkles of worry are rubbed away. Shadows of shame and doubt become portraits of grace and trust. He relaxes clenched jaws and smoothes furrowed brows. His touch can remove the bags of exhaustion from beneath the eyes and turn tears of despair into tears of peace. How?... God's plan is [simple]. He changes our faces through worship.

JULY 3

JUST LIKE JESUS

God, examine me and know my heart; test me and know my nervous thoughts.

PSALM 139:23

*I*magine considering every moment as a potential time of communion with God.... By giving God your whispering thoughts, the common becomes uncommon. Simple phrases such as "Thank you, Father," "Be sovereign in this hour, O Lord," "You are my resting place, Jesus" can turn a commute into a pilgrimage. You needn't leave your office or kneel in your kitchen. Just pray where you are. Let the kitchen become a cathedral or the classroom a chapel. Give God your whispering thoughts.

JULY 2

WHEN GOD WHISPERS YOUR NAME

Wait for the Lord, and he will make things right.

PROVERBS 20:22

Some of you are rehashing the same hurt every chance you get with anyone who will listen. For you, I have this question: Who made you God?... "Vengeance is Mine," God declared. "I will repay" (Hebrews 10:30 NKJV). Judgment is God's job. To assume otherwise is to assume God can't do it. Revenge is irreverent.... To forgive someone is to display reverence. Forgiveness is not saying the one who hurt you was right. Forgiveness is stating that God is faithful and he will do what is right.

JULY 1